HV
8138
S6

Smith, Ralph Lee

The tarnished badge

FEB 19 '80

MAR 16 '82

**Lake Tahoe Community College
Learning Resources Center
So. Lake Tahoe, CA 95702**

The
Tarnished
Badge

Books by the author

THE HEALTH HUCKSTERS

THE BARGAIN HUCKSTERS

THE TARNISHED BADGE

THE TARNISHED BADGE

Ralph Lee Smith

THOMAS Y. CROWELL COMPANY
New York
Established 1834

19283

LAKE TAHOE COMMUNITY COLLEGE

LEARNING RESOURCES CENTER

Copyright © 1965 by Ralph Lee Smith

All rights reserved. No part of this book may
be reproduced in any form, except by a reviewer,
without the permission of the publisher.

Designed by Judith Barry

Manufactured in the United States of America
by Vail-Ballou Press, Inc., Binghamton, N. Y.

Library of Congress Catalog Card No. 65-12507

Second Printing, March 1965

Preface

If you have opened this book in search of fantastic stories of corruption, I do not think you will be disappointed. But if you have picked it up to confirm the widespread American prejudice against police, you *will* be disappointed. The author does not share that prejudice, and nothing in his probing of police scandals confirmed it.

In fact, there is no harm in revealing at the outset one of the things I came to believe as I studied police scandals. This book is not the story of bad police in a virtuous society. It seems to me that the American image of the police as stupid and corrupt is a rationalization, as convenient as it is false, for the deep failures of civic responsibility that the police scandals have so shockingly revealed. No less than a revolution must take place in police work to bring it into line with the needs of modern society. That revolution has begun—thanks in great part to long-overdue public interest generated by the scandals. But even at its present inadequate level, most communities are getting better police performance than they really have a right to expect. As I went from city to city studying the corruption of law enforcement, I realized that I was writing a disturbing epilogue to Lincoln Steffens' *The Shame of the Cities.* Today, when comfortable complacency has settled into the suburbs as well as the cities, such an epilogue can only be called "The Shame of the Nation."

Since the end of World War II a wave of police scandals has erupted throughout the United States. On the basis of what I learned while writing this book, I predict that the end is not in sight. At this writing the lid is barely off the situations in New York and Boston. In other cities the lid has not come off at all. But there is little doubt that it will.

Instead of reacting with simple indignation to the phenomenon of policemen involved in crime, it seemed worthwhile to understand why it has happened. In this book I have told the story of what happened in some of the biggest of the scandals of the 1960's, and have set forth what I could learn and understand about why they occurred.

In writing this book I pondered the question of whether to use the correct names of police officers implicated in scandals. I decided not to. For one thing, indictments in some cases are still pending. In other cases, convictions have been appealed, and it will probably take years for the last of these cases to wend its way through the courts. The possibility of reversal of conviction always exists, and I have thought it best to give the accused man every benefit of the doubt. For another thing, few criminals suffer so drastically for their wrongdoing as police officers caught in the commission of crimes. Far more than other criminals, they are looked upon as betrayers of a trust, and a lifetime hardly serves to erase the stigma. "Police officers discharged for dishonesty have difficulty in securing employment," says Thomas N. Ryan, director of the Internal Investigation Division of the Chicago Police Department, in the understatement of the year. It seemed unjust that I should add to what has already happened to these men, and even more importantly, to their families. The names of policemen implicated in the crimes described in this book have therefore been disguised.

Contents

CHAPTER ONE

Criminals in Blue

In Denver, thirty members of the police force ran a half-million-dollar burglary ring. When the scandal erupted, a reform police chief was brought in. He was later thrown out of office by the voters.

In Buffalo, multimillion-dollar gambling and prostitution operations flourished while police issued thousands of "courtesy cards" to persons who included top men in the crime syndicate.

In wealthy Westchester County, New York, the commuters live comfortably with a vast crime ring that has "reached," and in some instances conquered, the local police. Discussion of the problem is taboo among most of the residents, many of whom work in New York City and like their hours at home to be comfortable.

In Indianapolis, twenty-two policemen were suspended for taking bribes while a reform of the department was in full swing.

In Boston, a nationwide TV program showed members of the Boston force circulating in and out of a known bookie joint. At the state level, a top official of the Massachusetts State Police has been twice indicted, along with more than a score of other top state officials and more than forty blue-chip companies with whom they were allegedly involved in bribery and conspiracy.

1

In Illinois, investigators found a little red book on the seat of a state police car. It indicated that ninety different trucking and construction companies were paying off troopers and officers of the Illinois State Police. The amount involved is thought to be half a million dollars.

In Chicago, police got a burglar to steal for them. They protected his "jobs" in exchange for part of the loot. When the burglar was captured and confessed, he couldn't get anyone to listen to his tale of involvement with the police. When the State attorney's office finally checked, four police vans were needed to haul away the loot found in the homes of seven of the cops.

These are some of the police crimes you will read about in this book. You will also read about the struggle against police corruption and the fight for better police work in America. It is a hard fight; victories such as the Indianapolis and Chicago reforms described in this book do not come easily, and in some cities the picture is one of failure rather than victory.

Police involvement in crime is a problem with a long history. Police forces grew and developed differently in the English-speaking world and on the European continent. The predominant Continental police tradition was French. From early Renaissance times the king of France had police. The force usually consisted of former soldiers. They were called *gens d'armes,* or "armed men." From the beginning, the gendarmerie was a national, centralized police force. Until recent times this gendarmerie functioned more often as the long arm of tyranny than as a guardian of the people. But when it did enter the modern era, it had much to teach the police forces that had grown up under the decentralized English tradition. Sir Robert Peel, in administering the English national police force (Scotland Yard) that was finally established by the Police

Bill of 1829, learned many constructive lessons from the French model, while avoiding its potential for excesses and abuse of power.

The English tradition—and the American, which drew from it—was markedly different. Until the late 1740's when Henry Fielding created his Bow Street Runners, England really had no police at all. Prior to Fielding's innovation, the country relied on the civilian-constable system that dated back to Norman times. The office of parish constable was unpaid and compulsory, somewhat like jury duty in our times. In each parish, residents were liable for constable service for a one-year period. The constables performed the duties of their office in such spare time as they had available or cared to give to the work. These duties included the apprehension of wrongdoers when arrest warrants had been issued. But, as can easily be imagined, this duty was rarely performed efficiently if at all.

As time went on, the duties of the constable became more numerous and more onerous to the officeholders. Those who found themselves in office hired deputies to carry out most or all of the functions. The money to pay these deputies came out of the constable's own pocket. Not too surprisingly, constables usually looked around for the man who would undertake the deputy's functions for the lowest fee. The search for bargain-basement law enforcement, typical of most American communities today, thus has an ancient lineage. Unfortunately, the results of trying to get something for nothing, or a great deal for very little, in the field of law enforcement are always the same, whether the locale be twentieth-century America or medieval England. It was hard to get good men to be deputies for the salary paid; and some of those who took the job supplemented their pittances with graft.

Other functionaries in the patchwork of old English

law enforcement were the justices of the peace. They were usually country gentlemen who offered their services on a voluntary basis to help keep the peace in their parishes. They received statutory authority in the fourteenth century, and after the Revolution of 1688 they were given substantial executive, judicial, and administrative powers. They were, in effect, a type of police magistrate, with greater powers to arrest, interrogate, release, and prosecute than any police magistrate has today.

When the JP's became powerful magistrates after 1688, constables became, for practical purposes, assistants to these magistrates. There were still no police as such. The system was creaky, and great crime rings began to grow up in London, fearing little from JP's and constables. The ancient system, based on the simpler needs of a more rural society, broke down in the face of the crime problems of a rapidly growing urban complex. Thus, another "modern" problem turns out to have a long history.

The problem was aggravated by the unpaid status of JP's and constables. To pay them, it was thought, would be unconstitutional. They therefore subsisted as a matter of course on unreasonable fees for services, on bail money that they were allowed to keep, and on bribes. In the infancy of the English law-enforcement system, strong bonds were forged between the law-enforcement officers and the criminal community.

Corruption of law enforcement was deepened by the prison system. Instead of being supervised by the state, which probably would have been bad enough, prisons were run by private persons who bought their positions or received them as lucrative livelihoods from the king. Like the constables and JP's, the prison-keepers and their wardens were unpaid. They lived on what they could extort from the prisoners. On arriving at the jail, the prisoner was greeted with the cheerful command "Pay or strip!"—meaning that he either paid a bribe to the keeper or surrendered his clothes. Heavy fetters were usually placed on all felons; the felon could get lighter fetters, or have them removed entirely, by paying the warden.

"A prisoner who could pay was given a private room with his own furniture and linen, and all the food and drink he wanted. In some prisons he could give parties for his friends from outside, and entertain his female friends in whatever way he liked. On the other hand, a prisoner without money would find himself down in the Hole with anything up to a hundred other unfortunates. The place was filthy, disease was rife, and the daily ration of food was a three-halfpenny loaf for a felon and a penny loaf for a debtor. All sorts went into the Hole, from murderers to children from the age of five. . . . Women and children of both sexes commonly sold their bodies to the warders and to more affluent prisoners for bread, so prisons were also brothels." *

The corruption and brutality of the system were only exceeded by its inefficiency. England had more than a hundred offenses punishable by death while France had only six, but neither the law's severity nor the terrors of the prison served to check crime. The reason was simple; in a big, sprawling city like London, without a police force, the chances of getting caught were not great. And, if caught, the chances of buying oneself off were good. The poorest and weakest were usually the ones that found themselves in the toils of the law. The powerful and strong remained free.

---

* Patrick Pringle, *Hue and Cry: The Story of Henry and John Fielding and Their Bow Street Runners* (New York, Morrow, 1955), p. 31.

Things rapidly became intolerable, so bold did the roving bands of thieves and cutthroats become. The government finally acted, but made the fatal error of making police work largely a matter of free enterprise. In 1693 Parliament passed an Act offering a reward of £40 for the capture of a highwayman who was subsequently convicted. In an open acknowledgment that the role of "thief-taker" would largely be assumed by fellow-criminals, the Act provided that the successful thief-taker receive, along with his £40, a pardon for his own offenses, if he was in need of one. The free-lance policeman also received the highwayman's horse, arms and money if these items were not held as stolen goods. The system was soon extended to offenses other than highway robbery, with a scale of fees based on the seriousness of the crime. Burglars and housebreakers brought £40 just like highwaymen, but a sheepstealer was only worth £10, and an army deserter a measly £1.*

The results of this legislation are not hard to imagine. Criminals were by far the largest class of thief-takers, and thus became the nation's only effective police. But they usually brought in weak, petty criminals, leaving the big gangs and the big operators alone. Since the fees were paid only on conviction, a man who brought in a big fish who was not convicted gained nothing but a mortally dangerous enemy. And if the big fish was convicted, his friends would take care of the presumptuous thief-catcher in the same way that Al Capone's friends took care of stool pigeons at a later date. Thus, big crime and the big gangs were hardly touched. Since any child over seven could be convicted of a felony, the thief-takers specialized in framing children and destitute people; these, along with minor criminals from whom the thief-takers had nothing to fear, were the

* Pringle, *Hue and Cry,* p. 35.

principal persons apprehended under the system. "The greatest criminals of this town are the officers of justice," said Horace Walpole in 1742, referring both to thief-takers and corrupt magistrates.

An important step forward in English police history took place when the novelist Henry Fielding was appointed justice of the peace in the Westminster section of London in 1748. He received the position because he was financially straitened, and his noble patrons had prevailed on the king to give him a post from which he, like other justices of the peace, could expect to extort a decent living in fees, bails, and bribes. Fielding, however, took his responsibilities seriously. From eighty constables under his jurisdiction Fielding selected seven that he could trust. These he attached to his magistrate's court in Bow Street, to function under the thief-catching laws, but as *arms of the magistrate's court*. Fielding then placed advertisements in the London newspapers, telling persons who had been victims of robberies or felonies to come immediately to his court, whence he would dispatch his swift thief-catchers to go out and bring in the crooks.

This was the first genuine police system that England ever had. In 1753 Fielding's "Bow Street Runners" scored great successes in bringing under control, for the first time, the criminal gangs that had openly roamed the streets of London. Fielding, by then an ill man, left London for Portugal early in 1754 and died there in October of that year. His blind half brother John, twenty years his junior, became the Westminster JP in Henry's place and continued the Bow Street Runners. Recognizing its great value, the Crown agreed to provide regular annual stipends to operate the system. Thus, an improved level and style of police work was brought about as a direct reaction to the problem of police involvement in crime. It is a pattern of action and reaction that prevails to the present day.

However, the system of court-attached thief-takers, while an improvement over the nearly complete absence of police protection that had formerly prevailed, was still inadequate to the needs of a great city. And, of course, outside London, in other cities and in the countryside, even this did not exist. Also, the system was only as honest as those who ran it, and few magistrates were as honest as Henry and John Fielding. By the nineteenth century these faults had become clear beyond doubt to enlightened persons. But proposals for a genuine police force brought reactions of doubt and fear. The experience of France, whose gendarmerie had a long record of being the foe of the people more often than their friend, caused England to hold back. And doubts as to the constitutionality of anything more formal than runners for magistrate's courts continued. After several attempts, the famous Police Bill of 1829 was finally passed. Under the guidance of Sir Robert Peel, the British police (Scotland Yard) began under an aura of integrity and a concept of limited powers and restraint that represented a great advance over the long-since-corrupted runners of Bow Street.

But all this came fifty years too late for America to benefit from it. The institutions of constable and justice of the peace were imported to the American colonies, where they served as the original backbone of such police protection as most areas and settlements had. Fear of a centralized police was at least as deep here as in England, if not deeper; even today America has no federal police force.

Thus, America imported the English precedent of underfinanced, understaffed law enforcement, and broke from the mother country before genuine reform was achieved in England. The special conditions of American life made a further contribution to the historical context in which police work in America arose. It was not until the 1890's, when the United States Census reported that most of the public grazing lands of the West had been "fenced in" under private ownership, that America's frontier days really ended. For nearly three centuries of its previous history, America had been busy taming its frontier. This created law-enforcement problems that are well known in American song and story.

I was an insatiable consumer of cowboy stories when I was a boy. I remember one in which a tall, silent fellow drifts into town, witnesses some gunplay, gets into the act, and rescues an old man from a gang of murderous rowdies. The city fathers press a sheriff's star on the newcomer and commission him to "clean up the town," which he does. He is then offered the job of sheriff permanently, but declines, saying, "You don't want a sheriff that some other sheriff might be looking for someday."

The story, of course, is as true as it can be. In many a frontier town in the West, the man with the fastest gun was made sheriff, to tame the other rowdies. Many Western lawmen were themselves lawbreakers, criminals, killers, and fugitives. The old system of using criminals as "thief-takers" enjoyed a new lease on life in the American West. The frontier itself was a vast asylum for fugitives of one kind or another. It was Western courtesy not to question a stranger about his past. "What was your name in the States?" asks a humorous Western folk song—expressing the assumption that when you left "the States" for the frontier, you of course changed your name for one reason or another.

Western novels usually fail to note that it was a simple matter to "buy the sheriff" in most Western towns. This situation led straight to a close tie between crime and the police as Western settlements grew into modern cities. Lou Blonger arrived in Denver in 1880, when he was a little over twenty and Denver was still a frontier town. He set up a saloon and dance hall, got involved in all kinds of schemes, and soon was king of the Denver underworld. From the beginning he paid off the police, and in time a private telephone line ran from Blonger's office to the office of the police chief. On Blonger's orders men were arrested or freed. By the 1920's he was a senior citizen of the town, in the "mining business," still deeply involved in dubious dealings with both the underworld and the police. The Denver force has yet to recover completely from the crippling effects of growing up under the thumb of a frontier crime ring. Anyone who doubts it should go on to chapters two and three of this book.

In other United States cities the development of powerful, corrupt political machines in the latter half of the nineteenth century was an evil omen for the police. Never strong and never free from the pressures of politics, police forces were among the easiest arms of municipal government for machine politicians to corrupt. The use of police forces for political patronage grew up in this era. Direct involvement of police in crime, with some of the proceeds going to political bosses, was also developed to the status of a high art.

In 1902 *McClure's Magazine* commissioned Lincoln Steffens to visit a number of major cities and look into the condition of their municipal governments. He produced a series of six articles that ran in *McClure's* beginning in October 1902 and were subsequently collected into an historic muckraking book, *The Shame of the Cities.* Police corruption, he said, is an evil that he found in most of the cities he visited, including St. Louis, Chicago, and Minneapolis. He devoted his full article on Minneapolis to the police scandal there. The article appeared in *McClure's* in January 1903 and created an immense sensation.

On January 7, 1901, Alfred Elisha Ames, M.D., a doctor with a long-time penchant for politics, took office as mayor of Minneapolis. He "laid plans," wrote Steffens, "to turn the city over to outlaws." For the position of chief of police Dr. Ames chose his brother, Fred W. Ames; for chief of detectives he chose Norman W. King, a former gambler with the necessary direct contacts with the underworld. In preparation for the great Operation Rakeoff, the mayor, his brother, and King checked over the roster of the police force, dismissed 107 of the best officers who could obviously not be trusted, and charged the rest of the 225-man force a fee for the privilege of being retained as policemen.

With the machinery all set up, Dr. Ames and his confederates opened the city to crime. Gambling, prostitution, pickpocketing, and cardsharping were all organized under the supervision of the detective division. Criminals from all over the country came to Minneapolis and negotiated with the city government for a "concession" in the town. Permission to operate could be obtained by paying a stipulated initial sum of $500 or $1,000 to the mayor, and making subsequent regular payoffs to the mayor and the police.

Perhaps the only thing more impressive than the bold confidence of this official crime ring is the way in which its activities parallel, detail for detail, the scandals described in this book, written more than sixty years later. Gambling went on openly, Steffens wrote, and "disorderly houses multiplied under the fostering care of Gardner," the officer appointed to supervise bawdy houses. Readers can compare this with the modern situation in Buffalo, described in chapter four. "Gardner even had a police baseball team, for whose games tickets were sold to people who had to buy them," said Steffens. Angelo Zuzolo, a shoe repairman in White Plains, New York, states in chapter six of this book that he always buys tickets for police functions when solicited by policemen. He never even bothers to take the tickets—"What I going to do with the ticket?" he said to the New York State Investigation Commission. Police burglaries, Steffens commented, were common. How many the police planned may never be known. Police captains and detectives were active in the robbery of a brewing company. They persuaded two men, one an employee, to learn the combination of the safe, open it, and clean it out one night, while the two officers stood guard outside. This sounds like a small-time version of the $35,000 cracking of the safe in the Safeway Supermarket by Denver policemen in June 1960, described in chapter two.

A grand jury dug to the bottom of the Minneapolis situation in 1902. Mayor Ames fled the state; Fred Ames and Norman King went to jail. Minneapolis got an interim mayor, Percy Jones. The gamblers promptly approached Jones and suggested a deal. No honest police force, the gamblers said, could handle crime unaided. But if Jones were willing to let certain gambling premises operate without police interference, the gamblers would use their connections and do their part to keep certain areas of crime under control. They were suggesting a "live and let live" arrangement that compares interestingly with the 1961 report of a Kansas City grand jury, describing the police situation in Kansas City, Missouri, in the 1950's:

Based on sworn testimony presented to this jury, it now seems apparent that sometime in 1953 a "deal" was made between the "syndicate" and certain members of the Kansas City, Missouri, Police Department which led to the "syndicate" being permitted to operate a number of gambling and after-hours liquor establishments, control prostitution, and fence stolen merchandise in Kansas City. In return the "syndicate" supposedly promised to commit no major robberies or burglaries within the city limits.

Police-syndicate "deals" continue today, especially in the newest breeding-ground of crime, the nation's suburbs. There a new page is being written in the old story of strong criminals and weak police forces. The situation is described in chapter six.

In the decades of the twentieth century following Steffens' exposé, police scandals erupted from time to time in United States cities. These often resulted in important reforms and advances in police work. Then as today, the most important initiative in raising the standards of the police profession came from within the ranks of the police themselves. The police expert August Vollmer surveyed many United States forces, and his recommendations served as the basis for improvement and modernization in many cities. But the dead weight of civic indifference was hard to overcome. By 1960, when a wave of new police scandals began to erupt. United States law enforcement as a whole was at least a generation behind the times, in terms of meeting the genuine needs of our society. The scandals have turned this festering problem into something that people can understand. Modernization of the police is now widely recognized as one of the most urgent issues in American life.

CHAPTER TWO

The Police-Burglars
of Denver

Shortly after midnight on the night of April 14, 1960, an unmarked police patrol car was cruising slowly through a dark alley in Denver, Colorado, with its lights out. Inside the car, Patrolman Lionel Murray and his partner, Patrolman Herbert Boyd, were chatting quietly and glancing at the dark doorways and back yards of the alley. Another routine night.

Suddenly two men materialized out of the shadows of a building, jumped into a parked car, and roared away. The police car gave chase. At the corner of Nineteenth and Market Streets a large, black object bounced out of the trunk of the fleeing car and fell into the street. Murray and Boyd continued to pursue the car, and half a block away they cut it off.

Two men stepped out of the car. One of them was Walter Lilly, a member of the Denver Police Force. The other was a man who was not personally known to Murray or Boyd. Lilly identified the stranger as a "former deputy sheriff" of a neighboring county.

Lilly and his accomplice re-entered their car and drove away. Patrolmen Murray and Boyd went back down the block and loaded the black object—a safe—into the trunk of the police cruiser. They brought it to headquarters, where it was soon identified as a safe that had just been stolen from the Alamo Coffee Shop, 1413 Seventeenth Street, in the rear of which the two men had emerged from the shadows.

It was three months before a full-scale investigation got under way. When the safe had fallen from the trunk it had knocked a license plate off the back of the getaway car and onto the street. This license, a Nebraska plate, had been lightly fastened to the car with bent paper clips. It had been picked up at the scene of the incident and was in the hands of the police. The police checked its registry, and found that it was originally issued to Walter Lilly's brother, George. George Lilly told police that he had given his brother permission to use the plate. Police said that he was not otherwise involved in the case, and he was released after questioning.

On August 3 Patrolman Walter Lilly was arrested. The story broke in the papers, and the case caused public shock and astonishment. Denver Safety Manager John Schooley, director of both the police and fire departments under the city's administrative setup, asked District Attorney Bert Keating to call a special grand jury to investigate reports of criminal activity in the Denver Police Department. At the same time he assured the people of Denver that Lilly was the only policeman then suspected of wrongdoing. "If there were any others, they would be in jail right now," he said in a newspaper interview.

However, there had been other reports, whisperings and rumors stretching back over many years. It was hard to avoid noticing that certain Denver policemen, when they retired, left the state to live in a style that would seem to be somewhat beyond the resources of a police pension, and in 1959 a full-fledged scandal erupted in suburban Arapahoe County, adjacent to Denver. A former Arapahoe County deputy sheriff named Robert Douglas had been arrested and convicted on burglary charges in Albany, Oregon, and was sentenced to two consecutive ten-year terms. In the hope of being granted leniency, Douglas offered to tell what he knew about a burglary ring that was being conducted out of the sheriff's office in Arapahoe County. He said that he had participated in it while he was a deputy sheriff there. His story led to the indictment of four active or former deputy sheriffs of Arapahoe County, along with a civilian fence and Douglas' stepson-in-law, in a burglary ring whose take was estimated at $100,000. Douglas also insisted that Denver policemen had been involved in certain of the thefts, and said that he had heard from them of still other crimes committed by Denver cops.

When Murray and Boyd first told Denver police brass that Lilly had identified his accomplice as a former deputy sheriff of a nearby county, it didn't seem to ring a bell in anybody's mind. But bells started ringing when Lilly was arrested and District Attorney Keating said that he was going to call a grand jury. Denver police got out pictures of the six indicted Arapahoe County deputies, and Murray and Boyd unhesitatingly picked out one of them, Ralph Donavan, as the man who had been with Lilly in the car.

In the meantime other things were happening. On September 18 Mrs. Jane Herzberg, an attractive blond divorcée who worked as a housekeeper for a Denver policeman, Henry Weslager, shot herself in Weslager's bedroom. The shooting was apparently accidental; Mrs. Herzberg, who soon recovered from the wound, explained that she was extremely frightened of guns and was unloading the service revolver in Weslager's room when the gun went off. The interesting part to Bob Whearley, Denver *Post* reporter covering the police scandal, was that the shooting was reported by Ralph Donavan, the man who had been identified as Lilly's partner in the getaway car. He had come to visit Weslager, who was not at home, and was standing on the porch talking to Weslager's son when they heard the shot inside. This odd stroke of luck revealed that Donavan and Weslager were friends.

The next month Whearley received an anonymous call at 3 A.M., telling him that it might be worthwhile to look into a business venture in town called Thor Car Wash. The next day Whearley looked up the firm's incorporation papers and found that two of the principals were Denver policemen. One of them was Patrolman Stuart Muzzey. The other was Patrolman David Maynard. Further investigation showed that Maynard and his brother James were principals in another business venture, Four Horsemen, Inc., a concern set up to operate restaurants and places of amusement. Where did low-paid Denver policemen get the money to operate such ventures, Whearley wondered as he wrote up the story.

On October 28 Lilly, vigorously maintaining his innocence, was convicted and was released on bail pending appeal. Suspended from the force, he began driving a Yellow cab. The grand jury indicted his accused accomplice Ralph Donavan on December 9—but that was about as far as the jury could get. Faced with a wall of silence, it gave up and concluded its hearings on December 16 with a report making general criticisms of the way in which the police department was being run. Few people believed that they had heard all there was to hear on the story, and Denverites settled down to an uneasy Christmas. Sure enough, the grand jury report was just ten days old when the rumbling volcano erupted anew.

On Christmas night Patrolmen Alfred Guerrero and

John Philpott were cruising in a police car in Aurora, a Denver suburb, when they noticed a parked Yellow cab with no passenger. The cab pulled away as the police car approached. Guerrero and Philpott sensed that something was up; they overtook the taxi and stopped it. The driver got out, walked back to the police car, and produced his driver's license. He was Walter Lilly.

The two policemen decided to search the cab. In the back seat they found $910.79 in cash, stuffed in a wastebasket. On the front seat was a loaded .25-caliber automatic; in the trunk were two crowbars, two chisels, a seventeen-inch screwdriver, a punch, and a steel rod. They placed Lilly under arrest. "I'll make it worth your while if you'll make a deal with me," Lilly desperately pleaded. But the two officers took him to jail.

The next morning it was discovered that nearly $1,000 —and the wastebasket—were missing from a drugstore near the spot where the two policemen had stopped Lilly in the cab. A six-count felony indictment was filed against Lilly by District Attorney Keating.

At first Lilly maintained his innocence in this as well as the case in which he had been convicted, but under questioning he finally wilted. He not only confessed his own guilt in both cases, but he spent four and a half hours telling the DA about eighteen burglaries in which he had been involved with other members of the Denver force.

The first week of January brought a wave of arrests. On New Year's Day three patrolmen were arrested on the basis of Lilly's accusation that they had been involved with him in eleven burglaries. On January 3 District Attorney Keating and Division Chief Walter Nelson quizzed Ralph Donavan after Donavan appeared in court to plead guilty to two of the six felony counts facing him. After talking to

Donavan they went out and arrested Patrolman William Goldman on suspicion of burglary. Goldman quickly made an oral confession and implicated two more Denver patrolmen in a $5,500 safe burglary at Denver's fashionable Flaming Pit Restaurant on December 20, 1959. The two men were Henry Weslager and David Maynard. They, in turn, were promptly arrested. On January 5 two more patrolmen, Louis Becker and Joseph Almond, were arrested. Almond was arrested because of discrepancies in answers he gave during routine questioning. Becker's case was more remarkable. Called in for routine questioning and under no suspicion, Becker apparently thought that the department had the goods on him and decided to cooperate. "Put me down for two," he announced when he walked into the detective bureau. The detectives promptly did.

In the meanwhile the police department was having a problem storing the cracked safes and other loot that were turning up all over Denver. On August 11 a pile of loot had been found in a junkyard. Another cache, worth about $5,000, was found a few days later in a deserted spot east of a highway out of Denver. In September two skindivers spotted a pile of loot that had been dumped into Clear Creek, along U.S. Route 6 west of Denver. It included an electric typewriter, four pistols, wristwatches, office machines, and cameras. On January 13 a small safe was fished out of the Platte River—it looked like one of three that had been cracked in the $22,000 burglary of a Denver discount house the preceding April 11. The as yet unidentified burglars had tunneled through a wall and had opened all three safes with consummate skill.

On January 15 another cracked safe turned up under a 20th Street viaduct. On January 18 the owner of a food market whose safe, containing $1,877, had been stolen, was asked to come to police headquarters to look over the cracked-safe collection. None of the ones he was shown was his, but he glanced into a corner and said, "That's it." He indicated a 24- by 18-inch strongbox with a broken lock. No one knew where the safe had come from, where it was found, or how it had ended up in the police building.

Several of the arrested men, out on bail, were rearrested and charged with additional crimes before the end of the month. Nine men had been caught in the net, and police officials assured the public that the scandal was at last in hand. But once again the furor had hardly died down before new arrests were made.

On March 8 three men were caught on the roof of a supermarket in Los Angeles and were arrested for attempted burglary. Two of them were civilians. The other was suspended Denver policeman Henry Weslager, free on bond, pending trial on the burglary charges in Denver.

All three were arrested. Only Weslager was able to make bail. According to the two civilians, Weslager and Patrolman Stuart Muzzey promised to raise money for the civilians' bail. "Weslager and Muzzey went to my wife and got $200," one of the civilians said. "Then my sister gave them $100. Those two split the money between them and left me in jail." The civilian was livid. "I thought if they could play this way, I could too!" he commented grimly. "We got a dirty deal from all our police friends." The two civilians had information on burglaries committed by Weslager and Patrolman Morton Ashley, who had already been arrested on other charges in January, and by Patrolman Stuart Muzzey. They turned State's evidence; Muzzey was arrested and new charges were filed against Weslager and Ashley.

On the morning of June 8 Morton Ashley won a directed verdict of acquittal on the original charges against him, when Lilly, brought up from Colorado State Penitentiary at Cañon City, broke down on the witness stand and refused to testify. "I am afraid of bodily injury at the penitentiary," Lilly told the court. It was later learned that, on the night of that same day, Ashley, back in business, participated in the robbery of a food market in nearby Adams County.

At that very moment even bigger things were brewing in Adams County. The fuse was about to be put into the powder keg that was destined finally to blow the Denver police scandal wide open. Early in June, Robert Sackett, operator of a private guard service called Western Patrol, received a visit from an old friend, Lincoln Kane. Kane had recently gone to work as a deputy in the office of the new Adams County sheriff, a handsome, popular ex-FBI man named Winston Fowler. He had noticed that Fowler's style of operation was odd. Some cases were thoroughly investigated while others seemed to be neglected. One day his suspicions were confirmed—he was approached about "making some easy money." Kane cold-shouldered the proposition. But later, in an action he was to regret bitterly, he accepted $500, representing half of a $1,000 payoff that a group of gamblers had slipped to the sheriff's office in exchange for permission to operate their gambling activity in the county without being raided. The other half of the money had gone into Sheriff Winston Fowler's pocket.

Now Kane had come to his friend Sackett for advice. Kane told Sackett that he was ready to come forward unsolicited and tell everything he knew about the sheriff's office operation, despite the fact that in so doing he would implicate himself in the gambling payoff. Among other things, Kane said, Winston Fowler was setting up burglaries for Denver policemen, and providing personal protection for the jobs by standing guard outside in a police car.

A few nights later Sackett hid in a closet in Kane's house and listened while Sheriff Fowler and several Denver policemen discussed with Kane their plans to crack the safe of the King Soopers supermarket in Commerce Town on June 29. Sackett felt that at this point there was only one agency left in the United States that he could really trust. With Kane's approval he went to the FBI.

The G-men could not officially enter such a local case, but they understood Sackett's and Kane's dilemma and provided planning and backing. Several trusted top officials in the Denver police force were contacted and let in on the secret. On the morning of the twenty-ninth these officials visited Richard Kuykendall, the twenty-nine-year-old chief of Commerce Town's seven-man police force, told him of the scheduled robbery, and worked out with him the full details for springing the trap. That night Chief Kuykendall called in an off-duty member of his force without previous notice and without telling him what was up. The two men entered the King Soopers market and hid in the darkness. A few blocks away, in a parked car, were a group of Denver police officers plus two FBI agents. The Denver officers couldn't cross the county line and the FBI men had no formal jurisdicion, but there was nothing wrong with being in a state of "watchful observation." Plans had been so carefully made that a tape-recording apparatus had been set up in the market, and Chief Kuykendall was in communication with the Denver officers and FBI men by walkie-talkie radio.

At 11 P.M. someone began to saw a hole in the roof of

the supermarket. The two police officers tensed. The sawing was quickly finished. Three men with handkerchiefs masking their faces dropped into the store, went quickly to the safe, and began to work on it. Guns in hand, Kuykendall and his assistant jumped from the shadows—Kuykendall shouted, "Hands up!" One of the men started to flee; Kuykendall fired into the air, and the man stopped. Another was carrying a .38 revolver; Kuykendall seized it from him. While he kept the men covered the other officer switched on the lights and removed their masks.

One of the men was Henry Weslager, free on bond and awaiting trial. Another was Stuart Muzzey, also free on bond and awaiting trial. The third was Allan Means, an active member of the Denver police force, who had not been implicated in any revelations that had so far been made.

Meanwhile, Denver *Post* reporter Bob Whearley had accumulated enough rumors and scraps of information to believe that the biggest part of the story still remained untouched. And he believed that it never *would* be touched as long as the police department and city officials of Denver were solely responsible for the housecleaning. After some reflection, he typed an eight-page memo to the assistant editor, Don Davis, setting down the whole skein of rumors and whisperings that had come his way—all the stuff that he had been gathering, but which he couldn't prove and which the paper therefore couldn't publish.

Three days later, while he was painting his house during a day off, Whearley got a phone call from Bill Hornby, managing editor of the *Post*. "Meet me at five o'clock in the governor's office," Hornby said.

Whearley put on a tie, drove to the statehouse, and was ushered into the private chambers of Colorado Governor

Steve McNichols. In the office were Bill Hornby and Alexis McKinney, assistant to Palmer Hoyt, editor and publisher of the *Post*. The governor was holding in his hand a copy of the memorandum that Whearley had written to Don Davis three days ago.

After a few minutes' discussion with Whearley, Governor McNichols made his decision: the state would step in. He appointed former FBI agent A. S. Reeder to head the state investigation, and Reeder picked Gene Brace, former chief investigator for the Jefferson County sheriff's office, as his assistant. Reeder and Brace set up an office in the statehouse and started to dig.

On July 22 Weslager, Maynard, and Almond were convicted in the Flaming Pit Restaurant burglary case. On October 9 Maynard and Weslager were to be sentenced and Almond was to have a probation hearing. Other cases were pending against Weslager and Maynard, and Muzzey and several others were awaiting trial. Things stood in this posture when Morton Ashley, acquitted on the original charges against him, was convicted on subsequent charges involving theft of $7,251 from the United States Loan Company in Denver. On September 15 he came before District Judge George McNamara for sentencing. When Lilly had been convicted he had received a relatively light two-to-four-year sentence. But Judge McNamara threw the book at Ashley—he sentenced him to four consecutive prison terms totaling thirty-two years.

Ashley was stunned. So were the convicted cop-burglars who were awaiting sentencing and the accused cops who were awaiting trial. They realized that the stiff sentence probably represented an official line.

The convicted and accused men pondered their situation. Some of them conferred on the possibility of turning

State's evidence in the hope of receiving lighter sentences. To do it would mean telling on many buddies still on the force, some or all of whom might otherwise never be caught. It was a hard decision. "If we talk at all," Maynard said to Weslager, "we'll have to tell everything." Weslager agreed.

Maynard's wife came out to see him in the county jail. "Dave, have you told them everything?" she asked. Maynard started to say yes—but he shook his head no. She looked at him for a long time, and there were tears in her eyes. "We can get by," she said. "We can still be a family when all this is over."

When she left, Maynard asked to see the warden. "Call in the state investigators," he said.

"After that," said one official, "it was standing room only in the confessional." Investigators Reeder and Brace worked late into the night taking depositions. Families of some of the men who were testifying received anonymous threats of assassination. The threatened families were moved to secret hiding places outside the city.

On September 30 Governor McNichols announced that he would hold a press conference. At the conference the governor sat grimly behind a battery of microphones with a prepared statement before him.

What I have to release is a most unpleasant revelation to be made to the good people of Colorado.

The investigation thus far absolutely certifies with corroboration that shocking and extensive criminal activities have for a considerable length of time been successfully carried on within the Denver City and County limits. This investigation has produced 206 statements, each duly executed, subscribed and sworn under oath. The 206 statements definitely implicate up to this time 18 additional officers of the Denver Police

Department in addition to the 13 presently under indictment and prosecution. There are three additional persons to be charged who are former policemen, and one additional individual not now nor formerly a member of the Police Department.* This investigation has disclosed 120 new offenses over and above those disclosed previously. Additional participants and offenses will unquestionably be disclosed as the multiplicity of leads are checked and verified.

This incredible criminal incest was spawned some years ago and became operative in the South Denver area by a group of policemen assigned there. Numerous burglaries and safecracking jobs were successfully performed. By virtue of certain interdepartmental transfers of personnel from the South Denver area three or four years ago, this police gang was split up and the members were transferred to the downtown district and other areas in the city. Immediately, new cells of crooked cops were formed around these old hands at the criminal game, and new members were recruited by the use of payrolls and loot splits.

A high degree of efficiency was attained by these gangs to the extent that one safe job was reported to have been completely executed in 17 minutes from start to finish. In most instances policemen together with their tools were delivered and picked up with police cars and the lookouts were uniformed police. Many locations were cased and surveyed in police cars, prior to the time the jobs were pulled.

In most instances, police reports were made out by the same officers who participated in the jobs. The same officers who pulled the jobs investigated their own robberies and removed incriminating evidence and fingerprints from the scene of the crime. Payoffs were made to officers stationed in the territories where the jobs were pulled.

The exact amounts of money obtained from these jobs is not known because police reports were not fully filled out. So

* This person was David Maynard's brother James.

many jobs were pulled that the offenders have forgotten some of the places and/or the amounts received.

After the governor finished speaking, fourteen of the newly charged men were marched up the marble steps of the statehouse and escorted to a room where they turned in their badges, belts, holsters, and police manuals. They were then led down the steps, past a battery of news photographers, and into a waiting paddy wagon.

When the governor spoke, the number of policemen implicated in the scandal was thirty-one. The investigation continued and the number rose to fifty-three. Hundreds of "unsolved" Denver crimes were solved. David Maynard was able to remember forty-three burglaries in which he participated. Stuart Muzzey confessed to thirty-nine. The total "take" of the burglary ring exceeded half a million dollars.

The cases went through the Denver courts for two years. Thirty men confessed or were convicted. In some cases Colorado's three-year statute of limitations ran out before the cases were brought to trial. In other cases, especially those brought to trial during the latter part of 1962 and during 1963, the juries voted for acquittal.

The stories that emerged from the testimony of the cop-burglars and from their interviews with Bob Whearley and other reporters kept Denver agog for months. One of the big cases was the safecracking job at Safeway Supermarket, planned and executed by Maynard, Weslager, and Muzzey. Maynard described it in an article entitled "I Was a Burglar with a Badge" that he later wrote for the *Saturday Evening Post*. By the time they pulled this job in 1960 all three were veterans. Muzzey had become a master planner, and Maynard and Weslager were probably the most skilled and experienced safecrackers in the nation. This job presented a special challenge. For months Weslager and Maynard had wanted to try their hand at cracking a particular type of safe—a Diebold 10—that was supposed to be burglarproof. The professional challenge was as interesting to them as the money. The local Safeway store had recently acquired a Diebold 10. One of the employees of the store had casually mentioned to a district patrolman that the store didn't send its cash to the bank—just its checks. The district patrolman, knowing of Maynard's and Weslager's desire to crack a Diebold 10, passed this interesting tidbit on to them. Maynard's brother James worked as a butcher for Safeway and knew the schedule of the armored truck that delivered money to the store. James also got a look at the inside of the giant safe and described it to his brother. It had three-inch-thick steel walls, he said.

The burglars held a planning session. Weslager drew a sketch of the safe from James's description, and he and Maynard discussed the best ways of attacking it. They decided that they needed more information, and they therefore planned a preliminary job at another market that had a Diebold 10, just to test their theories and to learn more about the safe's construction.

The preliminary job was pulled; Weslager and Maynard failed to crack the safe after working on it for three hours, but they learned what they needed to know about how the safe worked. They soon found from official police reports that they had come within a quarter of an inch of drilling it perfectly.

Another planning session was held. They decided to crack the Safeway safe on the night of June 29, 1960, just before the long Fourth of July weekend, when it would be loaded with cash. They planned the break-in for midnight.

The policeman driving the patrol car in that area promised them "coverage" until 3:30 A.M. when he went off duty. His coverage would simply consist of staying away from the area of the store during the three-and-a-half-hour period. He couldn't do more than that for them because his partner in the police cruiser wasn't in on the job.

At midnight, Maynard, Weslager, Muzzey, and Maynard's brother James pulled up at the store. While James waited in the car, the three policemen stepped out with equipment that included a big electric saw, a sledge hammer, and a portable police radio tuned to the call frequency so they would know if any alarm were broadcast. Maynard opened the front door almost effortlessly with a pry bar. They entered the store, pulled the door shut behind them, and made for the safe. Muzzey went to the mezzanine to act as lookout while Weslager plugged in the electric saw, and he and Maynard took turns at the slow work of cutting a pie-shaped wedge at just the right spot in the door of the safe.

They had six special saw blades with them. At 1 A.M. the first blade broke while they were still on the first cut of the pie. By 2 A.M. another blade had broken, and they weren't halfway through. Three more blades broke in quick succession. They fitted their sixth and last blade into the saw, crossed their fingers, and started on the last side of the triangle. At 3 A.M., when they were within an inch of completing the final cut, the last blade broke. Weslager picked up the sledge hanner and struck the pie-shaped wedge with all the strength in his powerful frame. The wedge broke off and tumbled into the safe.

Weslager knelt down, inserted a dentist's mirror into the hole, and studied the mechanism. The rest, he realized, would be easy. With the sledge hammer they struck off the outside dial and punched in the locking shaft. Weslager reached in with surgeon's hands and manipulated the mechanism while Maynard turned the big wheel on the front of the safe. The door swung open.

Inside they found drawers from the cash registers, containing several thousand dollars, and two smaller internal safes. It was now past 3:30; their "cover" was gone and delivery trucks would soon be arriving. They had to hurry. While Weslager scooped up the money from the register drawers Maynard swiftly cracked one of the two internal safes. It was crammed with fives, tens, and twenties, which they stuffed into a bag.

To manipulate the mechanism inside the safe door Weslager had removed his glove. They therefore went to the dairy department, got some cartons of chocolate milk, and sloshed it into the safe to obliterate fingerprints.

From this job the conspirators got $35,000—some of which was ultimately to become the capitalization of Thor Car Wash.

The last case in the great scandal was processed by a weary city in September 1963, more than three years after Patrolman Lilly was arrested. Ghosts still linger. To this day a number of big safecracking jobs that took place in Denver during the past decade remain unsolved. All the men convicted in the scandal except one were patrolmen, and that one was a sergeant. No one with the rank of lieutenant or higher was convicted or even charged. Many Denverites wondered how such a large, smoothly coordinated, successful crime ring could ever have operated without a single commissioned officer in the department having any knowledge of it.

CHAPTER THREE

Denver —Action and Reaction

Early in 1964 I had lunch at the Brown Palace Hotel, one of Denver's famous old landmarks, which carefully preserves the atmosphere of Victorian splendor that characterized the fancier saloons, dance halls, and hotels of the city's frontier past. My host was one of the most prominent civic leaders of Denver.

"The fact of police corruption was pretty well known before the scandal broke," he said to me over cocktails. "From time to time there had been rumblings, and district attorneys made occasional inquiries. It was just a washing out of overalls—it didn't get down to the underwear. Police corruption was simply accepted as part of the city's way of life. Many people felt 'As long as their hand isn't in *my* pocket, I don't care.' "

My host signaled the waiter for another drink. "We had a fellow in our office," he said, "who joined our staff after spending several years on the Denver force. This fellow used to tell me that if you were on the force you had to decide which group you were in. Nobody required you to join the burglars. You could be in the good group, if you wanted to. But if you *did* decide to go with the good group, there was one commandment you followed. You didn't rat on the guys that you knew were in the bad group.

"When the scandal broke, I didn't observe that many people around town were really too upset. It wasn't until it became a national story and the state of Colorado stepped in that any large number of people really began to feel uneasy.

"That's the kind of place Denver is. Take the situation with the Better Business Bureau. There was a Better Business Bureau here for about three years in the late 1920's and then it folded. For twenty years efforts were made to get a new bureau going here, but the merchants opposed it. They were very comfortable just the way they were. We didn't finally get another Better Business Bureau until the 1950's, and it still is not strongly supported."

I interviewed this man while studying the aftermath of the Denver scandal. Police Chief James Childers, whose personal integrity was never questioned, resigned. The city council authorized $20,000 to bring in an eight-man survey team of expert consultants from the International Association of Chiefs of Police. This team was to spend four months reviewing the entire operation of the Denver Police Department and make comprehensive proposals for change and modernization. Such surveys are an important recent development in police work in the United States; their genesis and importance are discussed in chapter seven.

The IACP sent a distinguished team to Denver, headed by Quinn Tamm, then director of the IACP's field services division, and now its executive director. Personnel selection and evaluation were studied by Stanley Schrotel, chief of the Cincinnati, Ohio, force, widely regarded by professionals as one of the best in the nation. Schrotel's detective chief, Henry Sandman, surveyed the Denver detective bureau. George O'Connor, director of training for the Chicago Police Department under its reform administration, studied the training program. IACP staff members on the team included Harwood Knight, who had just spent two years helping to install the Chicago Police Department's computer system, which is described in chapter ten.

As one of its first acts, the survey team was asked by Mayor Batterton and the Denver city council to recommend a police executive of national stature to become chief of police in Denver. The team recommended James Slavin, chief of the Kalamazoo, Michigan, force. Slavin, a 1946 graduate of the Traffic Institute at Northwestern University, was assistant director of training in police administration at the Traffic Institute from 1948 to 1957, when he left to become police chief of Kalamazoo. He had done a distinguished job with the Kalamazoo force and had earned the respect of his peers as one of the best of the all-too-rare modern breed of police executives. He was offered the Denver job and accepted it, taking over the reins in January 1962.

On February 7 Chief Slavin was the honored guest of the City Club of Denver at a luncheon at the Brown Palace. Slavin told the civic leaders that major changes would soon be made in the Denver department on the basis of the IACP team's recommendations. As to how the scandals came about, Slavin spoke calmly and firmly: "It is impossible for me to believe that what happened within the department was out of context with the morals of the rest of the comunity." Some observers believe that the city of Denver was reluctant to forgive Slavin for this expression of opinion.

Meanwhile various members of the IACP team were completing their findings. Stanley Schrotel finished his part of the job at the end of January and returned to Cincinnati.

There he made some informal remarks to the newspaper-men about the Denver problem. "Inadequate training, lack of experience, and a tendency to sweep dirt under the rug," was his succinct summary of the causes of the scandal. Denver personnel "from recruits on up" showed "alarming lack of training."

Slavin, meanwhile, had been talking to his men. "Together we will make this a department of which Denver can be proud," he said. "We have to change the police department and we can't expect the public to do it."

The initial reaction of many men on the force to Slavin was obviously favorable. "Friday morning the police station was buzzing with words of praise and confidence in the soft-spoken chief," the Denver *Post* reported. "One officer said, 'He seems tough but fair, and that's just what we need.'"

On February 8 the first major overhaul of the department was begun. An existing bureau of internal affairs was expanded to deal with complaints of police corruption. Its main functions were to clear the innocent, establish the guilt of wrongdoers, and facilitate prompt and just disciplinary action. Five men were assigned to the bureau. Although smaller than the Chicago department's internal investigation bureau described in chapter eleven, its function was the same. In the two cities, this building block of reform experienced very different fates.

Next Slavin turned to another IACP recommendation, the establishment of a planning bureau. The Denver force had no formal apparatus for planning. Analysis of crime patterns, marshaling of forces to meet these patterns, review of procedures, and control of finances are functions which, in a modern police department, are handled by a bureau whose whole concern is planning. Chapters seven and ten describe modern planning operations in action in a medium-sized city, Indianapolis, and a large city, Chicago. Slavin set up a planning bureau in the Denver force similar to the one that has been used so successfully in Indianapolis.

On April 1 the IACP team recommended sharp increases in police pay scales in Denver. A starting salary of $500 a month, instead of the $388 a month then in effect, was recommended, and raises were recommended in all other grades. Slavin promptly sought a charter amendment to implement these proposals.

Throughout the winter and spring, Slavin worked hard on reorganization. Three new division chiefs were appointed, men were reassigned, and technicians were named to staff new departments and establish new functions. Denver was beginning to have a modern police force.

The IACP's final reports were issued in June and July. The June report was a stinging criticism of the operation and management of the Denver department under the old setup. The report contained detailed recommendations regarding supervisory personnel, restructuring of the force, and tightening up of command responsibility. The July report made equally sweeping criticisms of the old styles of recruitment, promotion, and disciplinary procedures. The IACP also criticized the assignment of detectives to noninvestigative work and other misuse of personnel.

But Slavin was already heading into shoal waters. For one thing, his calm, mild manner was more a disadvantage than an advantage in the rough-and-tumble world of Denver politics. Slavin, to many, was the incarnation of the egghead moving into a field where eggheadism was less useful than old-fashioned toughness.

By early 1963 the opposition had crystallized and the

battle lines had formed. Mayor Batterton's opponent in the 1963 mayoralty election was Thomas Currigan, who rallied the anti-Slavin forces to his banner. Currigan supporters charged that Slavin had too mild a manner to do police work effectively, and had shown himself incompetent to run the department. Currigan made it clear to Denver voters that his first action, if he were elected, would be to fire Chief Slavin and put a different kind of man in charge of Denver police. It was a key issue—probably *the* key issue—of the campaign. On election day, June 19, 1963, Currigan received 78,878 votes to 58,153 for incumbent Batterton. The next day Slavin announced that he would resign effective June 30. He returned to Northwestern University, where he is now associate director of the Traffic Institute.

Two days before his July 7 inauguration, Mayor-elect Thomas Currigan chose a relatively unknown twenty-nine-year-old lawyer, Daniel S. Hoffman, to succeed John Schooley as safety manager, to run the police and fire departments. The next day he announced that Captain Harold A. Dill would succeed Slavin as chief of police.

In November 1951 Captain Dill had taken charge of the South Denver district. He was in charge of it throughout the 1950's while the great police burglary ring was being spawned within the district. Dill was never personally implicated in the criminal activity and no one holds him responsible as the commanding officer of the police burglars. Captain Dill is a "public personality" with a ready facility for making friends and political allies. South Denver liked him. When he was reassigned to police headquarters in 1960 a delegation from the South Denver Civic Association visited Schooley and pleaded with him in vain to dissuade him from removing Dill from South Denver.

Under Slavin's reorganization Dill had been assigned to the wardenship of the city jail.

A week after Currigan's inauguration, the new mayor and Safety Director Hoffman issued a joint statement saying that they would "keep in close touch with the police department." Dill said that he was pleased. "It indicates that they are standing up for our system and plugging for us," he stated. "That hasn't happened before." At this juncture, Chief Dill was already reorganizing the just-reorganized department. Much of the $20,000 worth of work by the IACP was to be junked. The internal affairs bureau, set up to investigate complaints of corruption, was cut back from five men to three, and two of these three were assigned additional duties. The planning bureau was scrapped. A twelve-man decoy squad assigned to combat muggers, purse-snatchers, and rapists was disbanded.

"We don't need planners," he said, explaining one phase of his program. "I do the planning. We need policemen. A big planning staff is fine for propaganda or press releases, but we can't afford those frills." He took a similar approach to the IACP's recommendations on training and recruiting. The IACP had recommended that new men be assigned to hand-picked field training officers who would serve as models of "the professional police officer dedicated to the concept of public service." "This isn't necessary," said Dill. "A rookie can learn from the stupidest man on the department. This emphasis on field training is only a crutch. You don't train integrity into people."

Captain Dill has put heavy emphasis on getting more patrolmen on the street, and increasing the number of sergeants and supervisory personnel. Increasing the number of supervisors is in line with the ICAP's recommendations, but his placing of more men on the beat has been largely achieved by elimination of IACP administrative recommendations. Everywhere, men were reassigned. Twelve of the force's sixteen police captains were put into new jobs. Of the thirty-eight technician appointments made by Slavin to meet IACP's recommendations, twenty-seven were scrapped by Dill because, he told a reporter, they were "political apointments made to subvert the civil service system." A few days later, sixty-two other officers were transferred and reassigned.

Denver is happy, especially South Denver. The South Denver Civic Association presented Dill its Grover Kenney Memorial Award for "outstanding achievement." Albert A. Melichar, chairman of the Association's Luncheon Committee, explained why Dill was getting the award: "He has built police morale and improved police work. He's a fine man. I've known him for twenty years." Mayor Currigan is equally enthusiastic. "In Harold Dill we have a policeman's policeman who knows the Denver situation," Currigan states. "It was almost like a New Year's Eve celebration in the Police Building when the word went out that he was going to replace Slavin. Dill is a chief in whom the people can place its confidence and trust."

When I called Chief Dill's office for an interview, the request was gladly granted. At the appointed hour I entered his office and found him sitting at his desk, impeccably dressed in the uniform of a Denver chief, with two gold stars on each collar. As we talked, Dill sat forward, relaxed, but alert. He dodged no questions and gave the impression of friendly firmness and immense political sagacity. From time to time deeper passions seemed to stir, especially on subjects relating to "bureaucracy." "The soft, fluffy jobs have been eliminated," he said. "This was something that had to be done." We touched on the question of scientific police investigation. Again his eyes sparkled. "The 'scientific police investigators' say that if you don't follow 'em you'd be sunk. It's not so." He is firmly opposed to what he calls "administrative complexity" in police work. "It creates little empires," he said. "If you try to be an administrator running police, you'll be killed. You have to have high sales resistance."

Chief Dill was anxious not to be recorded as critical of the previous administration, and he never deprecated his predecessor. "I don't disagree with him," said Dill. "He was a nice person and a good administrator."

Many leading United States law-enforcement experts take a dim view of what has happened in Denver. "Denver doesn't want good law enforcement" is a comment I heard five or six times. This is an oversimplification. Chief Dill *does* want good law enforcement and works very hard to achieve it. He simply believes that it is not to be found in the aspects of modern criminology and police administration that he eliminated when he took office.

The Dill-Slavin controversy is a drama that is enacted, in one form or another, whenever a city attempts a comprehensive modernization of its police. A survey is usually conducted, and the survey team recommends changes in line with modern concepts of criminology and police administration. A reform administration in the department goes to work to put the recommendations into effect. Inevitably, it encounters resistance. At this juncture the presence or absence of community support can determine whether or not the modernization program is carried through. In Indianapolis, as described in chapter seven, powerful forces resisted the implementing of the survey team's recommendations, but there the unwavering backing of the public and the city's political leaders gave the reformers the support they needed to complete the program.

In Chicago, events ran a similar pattern. As we shall see, Chicago's great scandal broke just four months before Denver Patrolmen Murray and Boyd picked up the safe that had fallen out of Lilly's car. Like Denver, Chicago got a new police head, Superintendent Orlando W. Wilson, and the experts were called in to help modernize the force. Wilson began to make changes and soon ran into the inevitable storms. The Chicago Patrolmen's Association opposed a change that Wilson wished to make in disciplinary procedures, and the issue quickly became a rallying point for antireformers. The CPA called a mass meeting, at which a representative of Mayor Daley was roughed up and hustled out of the hall while several thousand patrolmen cheered a speech by their leader, denouncing Wilson and calling for his scalp.

But Mayor Daley and the civic leaders and people of Chicago united behind Wilson. The police superintendent was made the subject of special attention and honors at every civic function and social gathering he attended. It soon became evident that within the great silent ranks of the force there was widespread support for Wilson, too. Even a majority of the rebellious patrolmen, after blowing off steam and working off their emotional opposition to the new ways, obviously had serious second thoughts. At the height of the controversy the gambling squad presented Wilson with a trophy for the improvement he had brought about in equipment and working conditions. A second "mass meeting" called by the CPA was attended by only a few hundred men, and the "get-Wilson" movement petered out.

CHAPTER FOUR

See Nothing, Know Nothing— The Police in Buffalo

Tastefully and conservatively dressed, demure and poised, Mary Keenan sat in the witness chair and answered every question calmly, quietly, and unflinchingly. Under subpoena by the New York State Investigation Commission in its 1960 investigation of the Buffalo Police Department, she was cooperating fully in open hearings in spite of threats of reprisals. As hushed spectators in the jam-packed Erie County courtroom strained to hear her soft voice, the city of Buffalo was facing its moment of truth.

Q. Did you make more money at Margaret's than you did at Mamie's?

A. Yes, sir, I did.

Q. Did you entertain more men at Margaret's?

A. Yes.

Q. How many men did you entertain at Margaret's house of prostitution on an average week?

A. Gee, I don't remember, but I know it was an awful lot . . .

Q. What would be a good day's profit for you at Margaret's house?

A. Gee, about $100 . . .

Q. Would you say you took part in the act of prostitution with as many men from the bars as you had in Margaret's or Mamie's or with more men?

A. I had more, but they were much better. They paid better.
Q. You had more men and they even paid better?
A. Yes.
Q. So that you would say that your earnings were more than $2,000 a week on good weeks?
A. Yes.

Buffalo is the principal city of the large metropolitan area in western New York State called the Niagara Frontier. This area, comprising the major industrial counties of Erie and Niagara, is growing swiftly under the impetus of the St. Lawrence Seaway and the Niagara Power Project. It has made Buffalo the second largest city in the state, with a population of over half a million.

Buffalo is a busy, cosmopolitan city and a popular convention center. Its uniformed police force numbers over 1,300 men, plus more than 300 civilian employees. The department's annual budget exceeds $8.3 million. As day followed day in the State Investigation Commission's hearings on law enforcement in Buffalo, the city learned what it was getting for its money.

The New York State Investigation Commission was set up for a five-year period in May 1958; its life was extended for two more years in 1963. It was designed to overcome gaps and deficiencies in ordinary government investigative machinery. Investigations conducted by legislative bodies are often partisan in nature and intent—when they are conducted at all. To meet this problem the New York State legislature created the long-term, nonpartisan investigation commission, giving to it subpoena powers and a roving assignment to seek out corruption. This has, for legislators, the merit of getting them off the hook. Organized crime, the relationship of crime to government, poor law enforcement, the conduct of public officials and employees—these are the kinds of hot potatoes that the commission was created to investigate.

In one of its first major projects the commission investigated syndicated gambling in central and western New York State. Its report, released in 1961, was a blockbuster. Highly organized professional gambling, it found, flourished in most major cities in the area and provided organized crime with its principal source of revenue. The commission located about one hundred distinct bookmaking operations, the average operation involving about ten persons. Its raids led to the arrest of 107 bookmakers, 54 of whom were found guilty and sentenced. The results of the investigation, said the SIC's report, "convinced the Commission that the total gross volume of bookmaking in the Central New York State area during 1959 could be said to have reached approximately one-half billion dollars, with a net profit to the bookmaking operators of not less than fifty million dollars." This major capital financing of American crime, the commission found, is carried on in an atmosphere of public indifference and with the active connivance of the police. In Buffalo the numbers racket and other forms of syndicated gambling were especially active. One SIC investigator asked a Buffalo policeman where he could play a number. The policeman directed him.

Working closely with the regional section of the criminal intelligence unit of the New York State Police under the supervision of Sgt. William Lombard, SIC investigators spotted major gambling operations in Buffalo. On Friday, October 23, 1959, at exactly 3 P.M., commission agents and state policemen walked in simultaneously on thirteen major gambling banks and thirteen bookmaking operations in Buffalo, showed their badges, and arrested fourteen flabbergasted bookmakers and forty-six policy operators. The operations were being run as if they were legitimate businesses, complete with phone operators and accountants with IBM calculating machines. Betting slips, account books, and thousands of dollars in cash were right out in the open. It was obvious that the last thing the syndicate expected was trouble from the police.

The testimony before the commission revealed that most of the arrested men had previous criminal records; many had spent relatively secure lifetimes in crime. Some were well-known syndicate gangsters and racketeers. Their close ties to the police were revealed by a remarkable bit of evidence. More than twenty "courtesy cards," issued by various fraternal organizations and clubs of Buffalo police, were seized from the arrested gamblers and gangsters. Most of the cards were in the possession of the top-echelon men who were masterminding the great numbers "banks." One was on indefinite probation for assaulting a Buffalo policeman; he nevertheless had in his possession a valid membership card in the Buffalo Police Department Motorcycle Club. "This is to certify," said the card, "that the bearer is an Honorary member of the Buffalo Motorcycle Division." Another top policy operator was carrying a membership card in the Buffalo Police Radar Club. A third, Joseph Occhino, was carrying—

(1) A police commissioner's card, signed by Buffalo Police Commissioner Frank N. Felicetta and giving him the "Courtesy of the Police Department";

(2) An honorary membership card in the Erie Club, the fraternal organization of the Buffalo Police Department;

(3) A valid membership card in the Motorcycle Club; and

(4) A membership card in the Buffalo Detective Ser-

geants and Detectives Association signed by Edward Wagner, assistant chief of Buffalo detectives, and reading, "Any courtesy shown to the bearer will be appreciated."

While conducting this investigation, the commission received complaints from the public about the Buffalo police. Reverend George J. Leake, pastor of the Durham Memorial African Methodist Episcopal Zion Church, complained that prostitution was so open in the city that women members of his congregation would be routinely approached on the street and asked if they were available for prostitution. "Respectable housewives going to church in the evening couldn't go to church without being bothered," he said. The situation was confirmed by commission investigators working on the gambling investigation. One of them was solicited by a prostitute in broad daylight right in front of the fourth precinct police station house. ("Sorry, sweetie," he said, "I'm busy!")

The commission decided to conduct a full-scale investigation of law enforcement in Buffalo. Some investigators went to Buffalo to work directly with state police and Buffalo police, while others assumed undercover identities, drifting into Buffalo and living in third-rate hotels and boardinghouses. One of the investigators, a talented accordionist, sought and secured occasional employment as an entertainer. He soon found himself rubbing elbows with Buffalo policemen at the bars of illegal after-hours speakeasys. The cops quaffed their drinks and paid no attention to prostitutes who were plying their trade within earshot.

Prostitution, the investigators found, was indeed right out in the open. "In the downtown areas," an investigator said, "it was just a simple matter of walking along the street, and prostitutes would approach you and give you their price, give you their phone number, give you their address, and would make open solicitations right on the street. There was no pretense, there was no effort to couch the solicitation in vague terms. It was a direct approach. The same thing—you could drive along that area, stop for a red light, and possibly as many as two or three would come out to the car, speak to you right through the window and make a direct approach again."

Several investigators, posing as businessmen who had just arrived in town, got into cabs and asked the drivers where the girls were. The drivers promptly drove them to houses of prostitution. The agents entered the houses and engaged in light banter with the several girls who were always present. "I went in," said one agent, "and several girls were sitting in the living room. I said to them, 'What's this, have you got a lot of old ladies here?' We all laughed, and I sat down and had drinks with them. Then I said, 'You gals are pretty good. I'll come back later with the boys.'" The agents found, through numerous such visits, that the houses of prostitution employed as many as four girls at a time and operated for eight to ten hours every night of the week.

Cab drivers got their slice of the pie. When questioned in private hearings, cab drivers were completely frank with the commission about their roles. One driver explained that the madams usually gave cab drivers five dollars for each customer delivered:

Q. Would you find that business would be increased when conventions were in town?
A. Oh, yes; absolutely; oh yes. To be truthful with you, we need to have more conventions. It's more than logical because they spend these big bucks.

Q. How many calls would you make, say, to the houses when a convention is in town?

A. Well, if you get a carload every time, it's five guys, so that's $25. . . . If you are a good man you are liable to go there four times.

The three principal houses of prostitution, the SIC said in its report, were those run by Mamie Harris, Mary Dunlop, and Margaret Tefferroa. Lines of taxicabs and cars would frequently be standing outside all three houses during busy evenings. Mamie Harris, a buxom, easy-going woman in her fifties, dressed up in her best jewels for her appearance at the commission's public hearings. Relaxed and jovial, she suffered "lapses of memory" when questioned on certain phases of operations, but corroborated many details of the commission's findings. She confirmed the frequent presence of taxicabs bringing customers:

Q. When cab drivers would bring customers, did they wait outside or did they leave?

A. Sometimes they left and sometimes they waited.

Q. Sometimes they waited for their fares to finish?

A. Yes.

Mamie told the commission that she had operated a house of prostitution continuously in Buffalo since 1938. From 1947 to 1957 she operated without interruption at one location, 57 Walnut Street. She changed locations about once a year between 1957 and 1960, but continued to enjoy good business without serious interruption.

Mary Dunlop told the commission that she had operated a house of prostitution at the same address, 612 Michigan Avenue, from 1922 to 1960. She had been arrested five times during this thirty-eight-year period; in each case the arrest was only a slight bother. The last arrest had occurred in 1953.

Margaret Tefferroa said that she had operated her house of prostitution at a single location, 384 North Division Street, from 1951 to 1960, suffering one arrest in 1952. It caused her no trouble and had no effect on her operations.

Mary Keenan's testimony added some informative dimensions to the situation. Yes, she said, policemen had visited the houses of prostitution in which she was working. She began working in Mamie Harris' house, and before she had been there a week, uniformed members of the Buffalo force had made two calls.

Q. Will you describe what happened the first time that police came to that house while you were working there?

A. Well, they just went in the back and they talked to her [Mamie Harris]. They didn't talk to me. . . .

Q. They identified themselves?

A. Yes.

Q. Showed their badges?

A. Yes.

Q. Did they ask for Mamie?

A. They asked for Mamie. And then the lady went into Mamie's room and got her. She was sleeping, and she made them go in the back room until Mamie got up and then Mamie went in there. I don't know what they were talking about.

Q. About how long did they stay?

A. . . . about twenty or thirty minutes.

Q. Were there any men present on either occasion?

A. Yes, sir, there were.

Q. On which occasion was that?

A. On both occasions.

Q. How many men were present, approximately?

A. Gee, I don't remember, but it was quite a few in the house.

The commission queried Mamie Harris about the police visits. "You told us that the police found customers sitting in your place . . . did they ask you who these men were and what they were doing there?" asked the counsel. "I said they was friends of mine," the imperturbable Mamie grinned.

The commission could not find out what kind of business, if any, the policemen transacted with Mamie. She didn't remember. The commission's report states that, after the SIC had summoned Margaret Tefferroa and Mamie Harris to testify at private hearings, Buffalo Police Commissioner Frank Felicetta ordered two members of the vice and liquor squad, one of them a lieutenant, to visit both madams and find out what kind of information the commission was seeking and getting. No such inquiries were directed by the Buffalo police to the commission itself. Nor were any of the houses of prostitution, which by this time had been identified in the press, made the subject of any suspect-premises reports or subjected to any police activity. The madams testified that their operations had continued with no police interruption after the commission's initial inquiries had been made public.

Commission investigators checked 14,080 daily and weekly suspect-premises reports filed by the city's sixteen precincts over a two-year period. Eight of the precincts reported no liquor, gambling, or prostitution violations for the entire period examined. In the entire set of reports not one suspect policy racket location was listed. Commission investigators had easily located seven major policy banks in Buffalo during this period. Studying the policy numbers slips and adding-machine tapes seized at four of these banks during the raids, commission accountants estimated conservatively that the gross annual dollar volume of these four alone was in excess of $6 million. During the period a profitable bookmaking operation had been conducted *within police headquarters* by Desk Lieutenant Norman Engel, a twenty-nine-year veteran of the force. Records and betting slips obtained by the commission showed that Engel's operation involved sums of $300 to $500 per day.

The SIC's report tells of an occasion when evidence of gambling walked right into a precinct station. A woman had played a winning number at Fred Perry's Restaurant, 375 William Street, a headquarters of the numbers racket. Fred Perry refused to pay off because he could not find the original slip and would not accept the woman's carbon copy. The woman threatened to take her complaint to the police. Fred Perry told her that he didn't care. She also contacted Marshall Miles, Pete Craig, and Bonny Kelly, all top policy operators, in an effort to collect her bet. She told Miles that she was going to the police. "What did he say?" the commission's counsel asked. "He said he didn't give a damn where I went," the woman replied.

The woman thereupon marched right into the fourth precinct police station with her numbers slip and asked for police help in collecting her bet. She handed the slip to the officer at the desk and told him that the operators of the game were Marshall Miles, Fred Perry, Bonny Kelly, and Pete Craig. The officer smiled and told her that she could be arrested for having such a slip. He then handed it back to her and let her go.

The persistent lady next took her complaint to police headquarters. There an inspector told her to renew her efforts to collect her bet with Perry. "Tell Fred Perry," the inspector advised, "that I said I don't like welshers."

The following morning, the gambling squad conducted

a "raid" on Fred Perry's Restaurant at 375 William Street. An advance tip on this raid was apparently passed on to Fred Perry. The woman, who was with the raiders, described what took place:

Q. Were there any numbers slips found or were there any arrests made at that time?
A. No.
Q. Had you been to that place at about 10:30 on other mornings, other than the morning that you were down there with the Gambling Squad?
A. Ever since I can remember.
Q. What had been the usual state of things around that place in regard to numbers activity on the ordinary day at about 10:30 in the morning?
A. There would be a crowd around there. They would be taking the numbers and collecting money and everything else.
Q. Would there be policy slips and everything else around?
A. Yes.
Q. When you went down there on this morning . . . there was nothing there; is that correct?
A. There was nothing back there at all.

Fred Perry was unimpressed by this show of police displeasure. The woman never did collect her bet.

Police seemed to be hard put to find any evidence of gambling. On October 22, 1959, gambling squad investigators, according to their records, made suspect-premises visits to two locations, 227 William Street and 375 William Street. They reported no gambling activity. The SIC's report says that these were among the fourteen premises raided by state police and commission investigators at 3 P.M. the next day. They found that 227 William Street was a thriving numbers bank and that 375 William Street was a big race horse policy drop. The state's raiders arrested the operators and carted off boxes full of evidence. Prior to that, the gambling squad had visited 227 William Street on August 18, 19, and 22. "No gambling activity," they reported. On August 22, 25, and 26, a commission investigator made numbers bets at that very location.

According to gambling squad records, over 16,000 visits were made by members of the squad to suspected premises over a two-year period. Ninety-eight percent of the reports filed on these visits said, "No activity." A total of 144 gambling arrests were made during the period, all for misdemeanors; the arrests caused not a ripple in the operation of the rackets. Delving through the bales of evidence seized in the raids, accountants for the commission estimated that on any given day of the year, on policy rackets alone, 3,560 persons were engaged in committing misdemeanors and 182 persons—the ringleaders—were engaged in committing felonies. This latter group was never touched by the police. They couldn't be touched, Commissioner Felicetta testified, despite the fact that their identities were well known. They were, he said, "people that we will never arrest, people that you will never arrest, because these people don't handle policy slips." While police alleged inability to deal with the problem, the SIC states that the syndicate raked off a $4.3 million profit from the $6.5 million annual policy volume in 1959, while paying a total of $4,100 in fines resulting from seventy-two misdemeanor arrests. The overhead cost could hardly have been less. During the same year, said the commission's report, bookmakers, taking bets on sporting events, netted approximately $10 million from their operations in Buffalo at an overhead cost of $5,785 in misdemeanor fines. In the fourth precinct, where gambling was heavily concentrated, the police seemed to have especially bad luck in finding anything. The captain and all the detectives of this precinct reported that they suspected only one premises for any kind of violation during the preceding two years—and the one suspected premises was a place where a crap game was being played.

At this point, the commission said in its report, the SIC wondered what might be revealed by a more comprehensive study of the department's records. The commission's staff therefore analyzed all Buffalo Police Department official records relating to the reporting and recording of crimes for a fourteen-month period. Thousands of complaint memoranda, precinct logs, and police messages were examined. The inspection included record books, card-index systems, and headquarters statistical reports and work sheets.

The Buffalo Police Department uses a central complaint index system, built on nationally approved procedures recommended by the FBI for reporting and recording crime. However, the SIC stated that proper procedures were rarely followed. Complaint memos were improperly filled out. Even the identity of the complainant and the location and nature of the complaint were not recorded on a great percentage of all the memos studied. Precinct logs contained cryptic phrases giving no information on the case. Follow-up reports to headquarters contained the same meaningless terms or were omitted altogether. It was obvious that this station house gobbledygook could be effectively used to conceal crimes and kill investigations. It could also distort statistics, creating the impression of a clean city and an effective department.

The commission's staff went beyond the reports and investigated a number of the complaints. Statistical samplings were made in four categories of crimes—burglaries.

larcenies, aggravated assaults, and robberies—that were susceptible to independent verification. Investigators identified, located, and interviewed the complaining parties and compared the information that they provided with the police records.

A total of 117 cases were investigated. Only thirty-two of this number—27 percent—were reported and recorded as crimes in the official records of the Buffalo Police Department. The other 73 percent had been quietly buried by the police.

Among them, said the SIC, was a jewel robbery of a pawn shop at 428 William Street. Opening his premises at 9 A.M., the manager found a large hole broken in the rear wall of the store. A jewelry display case had been emptied of its contents, and jewelry valued at $4,000 had been stolen. The manager called police headquarters, and the police responded immediately. Officers interviewed the manager, received a fully itemized list of the stolen property, and took personal notes on their findings. However, the complaint memo on this crime contained only the notation "See complainant" in the space allotted for recording the nature and details of the complaint. The complaint log of the fourth precinct, where the crime occurred, bears the same entry. Under the column entitled "Report of Action Taken," the entry reads "Satisfied." No message was sent to headquarters reporting the crime. This $4,000 burglary was therefore never recorded, indexed, or counted as a crime statistic. And, of course, nothing else was ever done about it.

Later the same day, the same precinct received another burglary report. An automobile tire dealer reported that a burglar had entered his premises by prying open a window and had stolen ten tires valued at over $100. Policemen who responded to the complaint filled out a complaint form with a flat statement: "No burglary." This crime, another felony, was never reported or recorded at headquarters. So far as the Buffalo police were concerned, it never happened.

In another case the complaint log of one precinct carried a final report of a burglary investigation: "Window broken accidentally." Commission investigators found that the show window of a store at 711 Main Street had been smashed by a thief who stole a tape recorder out of the display. As with the other crimes, the books were quietly closed on this case with no action and no report of a crime committed.

Examining policemen and desk officers at private hearings, the commission discovered that, while concealing crimes in official records, policemen were privately retaining the real facts about them in little books called "Pittsburgh books"—a wry suggestion that the crimes were committed not in Buffalo but in far-away Pittsburgh. They thereby avoided the obligation of further investigation and reports which attend crimes that are officially reported and forwarded to headquarters. At the same time they retained the necessary facts to discuss the cases with insurance adjusters. A desk lieutenant at headquarters told the commission that fifteen to twenty requests for crime verifications a week were received from insurance companies. In most cases the requests were referred to the precinct involved, since headquarters had no record of the crimes in question. At the public hearings the chief of the communications bureau was queried about an entry in the "Action Taken" column of the third precinct complaint log, "Note in Pitt. Book":

Q. Didn't you testify that you have heard, or you are familiar with the expression "Pittsburgh Book"?

A. I have heard the expression, yes.

Q. "Pittsburgh Book," the very term, the use of it, connotes a crime-burying device, is that correct?

A. If a crime had occurred and if such a notation was made.

Q. And if it were made in the "Pittsburgh Book," it was buried?

A. If it was a crime, yes.

Q. Does that entry mean to you, sir, that there was a Pittsburgh Book being kept in the third precinct?

A. From that I would say yes.

Q. If they were keeping that in the third precinct, would that be fair evidence to you that they were concealing or burying crime reports in the third precinct?

A. I would have to say yes.

For obvious reasons, syndicated crime had apparently chosen Buffalo as a "good town." Seven of the underworld kingpins who attended the famous crime conference at the home of Joseph Barbara in Apalachin, New York (which is in the eastern, not the western, part of the state), were from the Buffalo area. They were the largest group from any single area of the nation except New York City. Studying the criminal intelligence setup of the Buffalo Police Department two and a half years after the meeting, the SIC found that the department did not have a file on any of these nationally famous syndicate mobsters—including John Montana, who was arrested at Apalachin a year after being honored as "Buffalo Man of the Year." Another Buffalo area mobster present at Apalachin was Stefano Magaddino. Buffalo Chief of Detectives John Whelan explained that no file was kept on him because he lived in Niagara Falls. The fact that he conducted most of his operations in Buffalo was apparently of no interest to the police.

Questioned more closely by the commission, Chief Whelan said that he maintained "personal files" on criminals, which were not the property of the department. He admitted that these were the only existing criminal intelligence files in the department. When the SIC examined these personal files, they were found to contain a few old mug shots, miscellaneous outdated criminal record sheets, and some old clippings from newspapers and detective magazines.

To combat organized crime, intelligence information concerning the specific identity, methods of operation, associations, places frequented, personal histories, and criminal backgrounds must be carefuly sought and acquired, filed, indexed, and studied. "Simply stated," said the commission's report, "the [Buffalo] department had no program against organized criminal activities, nor did it systematically gather and organize intelligence data. . . . Deplorable as it may be, the Buffalo Police Department, one of this nation's largest metropolitan forces, offered the Buffalo public no planned attack on organized crime, and lacked rudimentary police tools to maintain even a totally defensive position regarding 'professional' criminal activities." Key officers in the department, the commission found, "demonstrated a marked lack of understanding for even the necessity of an organized criminal intelligence program, let alone the scope of such a program of the professional competence to place it into effect." Captain Shanahan of the fourth precinct, asked if he kept intelligence information on known hoodlums in his precinct, replied, "Where would you get it from?"

Effectiveness of police work was further reduced—if that were possible—by the widespread issuance of courtesy cards to private citizens. The possession of police courtesy cards by a number of Buffalo racketeers rounded up during the commission's gambling investigation was one of the factors that had led the commission to take on its investigation of the Buffalo force. There is little question that holders of such cards can often expect special consideration from policemen when they break the law—whether the offense be going through a red light or running a multi-million-dollar prostitution or gambling empire.

The Erie Club, the police fraternal association to which nearly every Buffalo policeman belongs, refused to give the commission information on how many cards it had printed for distribution. The same was true of the Detective Sergeants and Detectives Association. The commission was also unable to get figures on the "City of Buffalo, Courtesy of the Police Department" card, printed for distribution by high-echelon police officers. The Motorcycle Club had printed 2,000 cards for distribution—each policeman-member received ten cards and could get more if he wanted them. The Police Lieutenants Association printed 4,000 cards, giving each member twenty-five and allowing him to have additional ones on request. The Traffic Men's Association, composed of traffic patrolmen, printed 1,000 cards. Between 500 and 600 "Traffic Safety" cards were printed for distribution by Francis Gaughan, director of traffic. The press run on the police commissioner's card, personally signed and distributed by Commissioner Frank N. Felicetta, was 2,000. The Radar Club, with a membership consisting of sixteen members of the Radar Squad, printed 2,000 cards.

A club of private citizens called "Troop R" also issued

courtesy cards. This club had donated $1,900 to the Radar Squad for the purchase of "elite" uniforms.

At the public hearings, Police Commissioner Felicetta was defiant on the subject of these cards. Asked whether he issued them, he replied:

A. I have them. I issue courtesy cards. I issued them last year. I issued them last year and I will issue them next year, if the Lord permits me.

Q. For what purpose?

A. For what purpose? For many reasons.

Q. I am waiting to hear the reasons.

A. Some people collect stamps, some people collect coins, and other people collect courtesy cards.

Among the collectors, as we have noted, was syndicate gambler Joseph Occhino. Felicetta steadfastly denied issuing a police commissioner's card to Occhino. The counsel then produced Occhino's card. Felicetta admitted that his signature and Occhino's name on the card were both in his handwriting. Felicetta had earlier admitted that, when he had been captain of the fourth precinct prior to becoming police commissioner, he had known Occhino to be a policy operator. The card had been issued within the past two years, long after Felicetta knew Occhino to be involved in criminal activity.

Interest among Buffalo policemen in doing a good job, seriously muted by the atmosphere in the department, seemed to be further harmed by political tampering. Buffalo Mayor Frank A. Sedita and his official family fervently denied that politics played a significant role in the appointment, promotion, demotion, and transfer of police officers. But sworn testimony of many high-echelon Buffalo police officers told another story.

"It would be naive to think that politics doesn't play a

part," Lt. Charles Ries, the gambling squad commander, testified. "There is no question about that; that's a matter of record. . . . When the Republicans were in, there was talk that they [detective promotions] had to be cleared with the Ellicott Square Building, and with the Democrats it was somewhere else."

A precinct captain, when asked if either political party was involved in influencing police appointments and promotions, grinned sourly. "I don't think that either party can run around with a white sheet over their head," he said. "It is just standard procedure that if one party happens to be in power, they will appoint ones in command who are of the same political affiliation."

One result was that no detective could feel secure in his job when the city administration changed, and few, under the circumstances, developed much devotion to their work. An inspector told the commission, "I know, when an administration changes there is usually a complete turnover in those districts—those positions in the detective bureau, and it may be that some men are reduced and replaced due to political reasons. That has been going on."

Another effect of the system was to overload the detective bureau, creating dangerous shortages in the foot patrol. This overloading was caused in part by political pressure exerted in behalf of police officers seeking transfer from a beat to the detective division. "Both political parties," another inspector explained, "like to have their friends taken care of."

All the men agreed that the situation undermines morale. "At the time of the municipal election and immediately thereafter," one officer explained in his testimony to the commission, "the force is in a state of—well, I would say, uneasiness, particularly the men in the detective bureau. They are uneasy as to whether they are going to be moved or demoted or replaced, and it's apparent to anybody in the police department that that fear is, in some instances, justified and the changes are made."

Among all the witnesses there was an attitude of complete resignation about the problem—a feeling that it had to be, and nothing would or could change it.

In addition to struggling in the jungle of political preferment, many men sought to increase their incomes by what was called second-front employment—a term dating back to the Second World War when policemen were allowed to hold second jobs in the interest of the war effort (in other cities this is usually called moonlighting). The practice continued after the war when police salaries fell farther and farther behind the rise in the cost of living.

Interviewing a substantial cross-section of the department, commission investigators found that 63.9 percent of those canvassed held second jobs outside the police department. The average number of combined police and second-front hours was sixty hours per week and a considerable percentage of the force worked a total of seventy to eighty hours a week. The effect on police efficiency was marked and drastic. At any given hour of the day or night a substantial portion of the force would be fatigued and would have little desire to maintain alertness or vigorous activity. Also, if an officer had to be at, say, a shoe store when it opened at 9 A.M. for his second-front job, he would be likely to avoid making arrests or performing investigative duties, such as pursuing indications of suspicious activity, during later hours of his duty tour, that might make him late for his daytime job. Alert police work is not likely to be performed if the predictable consequences of overrunning one's formal hours, or appearing at the DA's office or in court that day or on some subsequent day, might conflict with one's second-front employment schedule. Commission investigators felt little doubt that second-front employment was one factor in the burial of crimes by the Buffalo police.

In some instances the hours of outside work overlapped with hours of police duty. Either the department or the private employer was being cheated, and almost surely it was the former. And other hazards were involved. For example, the SIC report says that twenty-two Buffalo police officers were found to be working as school bus drivers in Kenmore, a suburb of Buffalo. In a typical situation the officer would work the midnight-to-8 A.M. shift as a policeman. Actually his duties as a bus driver required him to report to the garage in Kenmore, be out on his route, and make his first stop at 7:50 A.M. After completing the morning route, the driver would have to report to the garage again at 2:30 P.M. to return the children from school. On some days the officer would then be required to report for police duty again at 5 P.M. and work until midnight—all in the same twenty-four-hour day. The dangers inherent in the situation to the schoolchildren—to say nothing of the effect of the arrangement on the officer's police work—hardly need comment. The police department and the Kenmore school district were both aware of the situation.

Citizen complaints about the conduct and performance of Buffalo police were of little avail. The investigation of such complaints is, officially, the duty of certain police inspectors. But many complaints never reached them; they were simply passed back down to the precincts involved without being referred to an inspector. The SIC states that the State Liquor Authority referred more than two dozen citizen complaints of liquor law violations to the Buffalo police commissioner. He forwarded them for "investigation" to the very precincts and detective squads mentioned in the allegations. Those accused of misconduct were assigned to investigate themselves. One complaint forwarded to the police commissioner by the Liquor Authority read:

An unidentified male telephoned this office on the above date, complaining that [the cited premises] employs a young woman, 28, seven nights a week, from 6:00 P.M. to 3:00 A.M. at regular pay. Premises is open after hours, gives drinks away to anyone, is not taking out Social Security, Unemployment Insurance, or anything from young woman's wage. Is permitting bets to be taken in daytime at bar, at tables, or in back room. It is useless to contact Precinct No. 5, as members from that precinct are in the premises after hours drinking.

The complaint was forwarded to the fifth precinct for investigation. The precinct reported that it knew of no evidence of the alleged violations.

The attitude of both the police department and the city administration of Buffalo to the commission's investigation was frequently hostile. In making its final report, the commission stated that "an atmosphere of hostility and resentment created by actions of the City administration and leaders of the Erie Club tended to impede the progress of [the] questioning" at the commission's private hearings. Many top police officials simply took the position that everything on the force was all right. Investigative work, they insisted, was good. "I think my detectives do a very thorough job," precinct Captain Shanahan said to the commission. After the investigation was completed, Mayor Sedita made a special television appearance, reassuring the people of Buffalo about their police force and condemning the commission's work, which he said was an attempt to discredit the city administration and the police.

In its report, the commission stated that law enforcement in Buffalo had substantially broken down, and that an "absolute see-nothing, know-nothing attitude toward enforcement" had afflicted all levels of the police. The problems, said the commission in conclusion, "must be dealt with vigorously, imaginatively, and with a firm purpose of accomplishment. But therein lies the crux of the entire problem. Recommendations, rules and orders are no better or more effective than the ability and imagination of the men charged with carrying them out."

CHAPTER FIVE

Getting Ahead in Syracuse

In February 1960, says the New York State Investigation Commission in its 1963 report on its investigation of the Syracuse Police Department, Detective William Guest of the Syracuse force was trying to get a promotion to detective sergeant. Believing that the path to promotion might lead through City Hall, he had a talk with Mayor Anthony A. Henninger. The discussion left Guest uncertain as to whether the mayor would actively push his promotion. He therefore decided to take his problem to the man who, Guest felt, could bring the kind of pressure that would count. On February 23 he kept an appointment at the New York Central Railroad station with Percy Harris, chief of the city's biggest gambling network. He explained his problem and asked for Harris' help. Harris promised to give it.

The next day Guest's superiors notified him that he was being promoted. Jubilant, he called Harris' home (the number was unlisted) and left a message with Percy Harris' wife, Alice. "Tell him everything was taken care of today," he said. "Tell him his pal got that job."

Percy soon got the message, and later the same day he discussed it on the phone with a friend. "I had to kind of move around with some of these fellows getting appointments, you see," he said. "That kept me rather busy. It was obvious that I could help out and I did." As an afterthought he added, "It was surprising that they would resort to me." To anyone who knew the real power structure in the city of Syracuse, however, there was nothing surprising about it.

So everybody was happy. Everybody, that is, except Detective George Emerson, who, according to the SIC report, had also been busy trying to swing a deal for a promotion. When he heard about Guest's promotion, he called Harris (everyone seemed to have the unlisted number). "I saw your old buddy got a promotion," he said to Harris. "I was not too happy . . . it should have been mine." Harris was soothing and reassuring; there was, Harris said, "another vacancy." They arranged to meet at the railroad station to talk the problem over. When they met, Emerson asked Harris to help him get a promotion too.

On the evening of February 28 Harris called Acting Captain of Detectives Samuel Hyneman at his home. Hyneman wasn't in; Harris left the message with Hyneman's wife that "P.H." had called. A little later he called again, and this time he talked to Hyneman. Following this phone conversation Hyneman left his house, and the two men met at the railroad station, where Harris seemed to conduct a good deal of his police business.

In hearings held in December 1962, the SIC, looking into the crime ring that had held Syracuse in its grip for more than a generation, tried to find out what business gambler Percy Harris had transacted with Acting Detective Chief Hyneman that night. Trying to pin down Hyneman and Harris was like trying to lay hands on a couple of slippery eels.

Regarding the purpose of the meeting, Harris told state

investigators that he had made the phone call simply to congratulate him on his recent appointment as detective chief. Under questioning, he admitted that he had never called Hyneman at his home before, and that he had left no message of congratulation with Hyneman's wife when he failed to catch Hyneman in on his first call. When he did reach Hyneman, Harris said, he explained that he was going away and would like to see Hyneman at the railroad station before he left. "I didn't think it was correct to congratulate him over the telephone," Harris explained.

Hyneman had a different explanation. He told the SIC that, a few days prior to his meeting with Harris at the railroad station, he had met Harris on the street and had asked him if he knew who was running the "Cuban roll," a form of gambling, in Syracuse. Harris replied that he did not know, but would find out. When Hyneman learned that someone who identified himself as P.H. had called him on the evening of the twenty-eighth, he assumed that it was Percy Harris because he had been expecting to hear from him about the Cuban roll. When Harris called a second time and reached Hyneman, Harris said that he was leaving for New York City, that he had something for Hyneman, and wanted to meet him at the railroad station. Hyneman told investigators that it was an appointment that he wanted to keep, and he went to the station to meet Harris.

As to what transpired when the two men met, Harris said that they just shook hands and that he had said to Hyneman, " 'Congratulations, happy for you,' or something to that effect." That was all that happened, Harris stated. The entire meeting had lasted "maybe three or four minutes," after which "he left and I left."

Hyneman's version was again different. He told the

commission that he arrived at the station at about 9:30 or 10:00 P.M., saw Harris standing outside, and went over to him. They exchanged greetings and Hyneman said, "Did you get that information for me?" Harris promptly walked away about six or eight feet, but then turned around and came back, saying to Hyneman, "Say, you didn't come down for your Christmas present this year." "I never did come after it this year or any other year, did I?" Hyneman replied. Again Harris started to walk away, and again he came back, "fumbling around in his pockets." "He was about to give you your Christmas present, I take it?" Commissioner Myles J. Lane asked Hyneman during the hearings. "I don't know if he was. I assumed that he was," Hyneman replied. "Why the hell don't you buy me a house?" Hyneman claims he said to Harris—which meant, Hyneman explained to the commission, "Why don't you go to hell?" At this point Harris turned around and walked away, and he didn't come back. Hyneman told the commission that he thought Harris was trying to trap him in some way, but could offer no explanation of why Harris would want to trap him. Despite his alleged suspicions of a trap, Hyneman never reported the meeting with Harris to his superiors.

After each man had given his version of the encounter, investigators produced the following transcript of the actual phone conversation that Hyneman and Harris had held on that night just before their meeting:

HYNEMAN: Hello.
HARRIS: Hello. P.H.
HYNEMAN: Yeah. How are you?
HARRIS: Fine. Yourself? Listen, can you come out a minute? Are you driving?
HYNEMAN: Yeah, but let's see. When are you going?

HARRIS: Oh, about ten-thirty.

HYNEMAN: Well, why don't you forget it?

HARRIS: No, no.

HYNEMAN: Yeah, do that. I'll be better satisfied.

HARRIS: No, you won't.

HYNEMAN: Yes, I will.

HARRIS: Now, listen to me.

HYNEMAN: What?

HARRIS: You won't see me for about a month.

HYNEMAN: That's okay.

HARRIS: Well, I'll get ahold of my friend then.

HYNEMAN: What?

HARRIS: I'll get ahold of my friend K.

HYNEMAN: No, don't.

HARRIS: Well, then, come on down by the station—by the railroad station.

HYNEMAN: No. I've got a—I've got a job to do, a taxi job to do.

HARRIS: Well, that won't be long.

HYNEMAN: Huh?

HARRIS: That won't be long. Come on. I'll meet you by the far
end.

HYNEMAN: Lookit, why don't you let it go, really I'd much
rather it be that way. I really would.

HARRIS: I don't think you're doing right now.

HYNEMAN: Yeah. Yes, I am.

HARRIS: Huh?

HYNEMAN: Yes, I am.

HARRIS: No, no, you're not, not after—not after you find out.
Yeah, come on. We can talk anyhow for a minute. I'll meet
you down by the far end of the taxi stand—of the other side
of the railroad station. You know where I mean?

HYNEMAN: Um-huh.

HARRIS: By the dining-room side. Not out in the street.

HYNEMAN: Gee, I hate to do it now. Why don't you let it go?

HARRIS: No. All right I'll talk with you then. I'll talk with you.
I want to say something to you.

HYNEMAN: Well, okay.
HARRIS: I'll meet you there in about how long?
HYNEMAN: Oh, it'll probably be about twenty minutes.
HARRIS: All right. Fine.
HYNEMAN: All right.
HARRIS: Bye.

After seeing this transcript both men acknowledged that this was the actual conversation they had had. Harris stuck to his original story that the purpose of the call and the meeting had been to congratulate Hyneman. He admitted that there had been no mention of congratulations in the phone call, and that Hyneman was reluctant to meet him, but said that he insisted on the meeting because he was so anxious to congratulate him. When asked what he meant when he told Hyneman, "No, you won't" after Hyneman said, ". . . forget it . . . I'll be better satisfied," Harris simply replied, "That I couldn't answer."

Hyneman, who had previously said that he wanted to keep the appointment because he wanted the information on the Cuban roll, now explained that he was reluctant to see Harris because the information "wasn't too important" and could have waited.

As to the identity of K, Harris insisted that he had really said G, meaning the recently promoted Detective Sergeant Guest. It was not explained why he was able to compel Hyneman to meet him by threatening him with contacting an officer whom Hyneman outranked. Hyneman vigorously denied having any knowledge of K's identity.

The only man with the initial K who outranked Hyneman on the force was Harold F. Kelly, chief of the Syracuse police.

No one is ever likely to know the full details of the relationship between Harris and Hyneman, or what the two men said to each other when they met that night. Several things, however, are clear. For one thing, Emerson got his promotion. For another thing, Guest and Emerson were both among the members of the Syracuse police force who received cash "gifts" from the Harrises. Third, certain areas of the city of Syracuse's business were being run in a way that included consultation with known criminals.

One morning shortly after Guest was promoted to detective sergeant, Patrolman James Sink and Detective Arthur F. Peck were cruising the downtown area in an unmarked patrol car. The driver of the car immediately in front of them stopped and double-parked with the engine running. While the car tied up traffic, someone ambled out of a nearby candy store and delivered a pile of policy gambling slips to the man at the wheel. As the unmarked police cruiser followed, the man repeated this performance at each of five or six policy betting locations. Sink and Peck stepped out of their car and put the man under arrest. His name, they found, was George Lennon; he was a policy collector for the Harris syndicate.

The next day the two policemen rode around the same area at the same time. They were astounded to see another man in another car going the same rounds and carrying out the same mission as the man they had arrested the previous day! They arrested this man too; he turned out to be Johnnie Reddick, another Harris employee.

"We were amazed at the boldness of both of them, in broad daylight, at noon, not even trying to park the car, but staying right in the street and the runners came out," said Detective Peck at the SIC's hearings. "We thought this fantastic at the time, to think that they could get away with such an obvious thing."

When the arrests were made, Guest was obviously displeased. According to the transcript of the SIC's hearings, he asked Peck why he had done it. Then he called the Harrises at their home. Percy was out of town; Guest discussed the bad news with Alice. Alice was angry. She wanted to know why the two arresting officers "couldn't be handled." Guest indicated to her that her two collectors had been pretty careless. He promised to find out what charges had been made against the men, and whether or not they had made any kind of a statement.

According to the testimony of Alice Harris, Guest said that he would "get ahold of Bill and find out what the case was all about." Did he mean Bill Wilstack, captain of the vice squad, Mrs. Harris was asked by the counsel for the State Investigation Commission. "I couldn't tell you," Mrs. Harris replied.

At one time, Wilstack had paid an "investigative visit" to the Onondaga Square Club, owned by the Harrises. According to Mrs. Harris, Wilstack apologized to William "Sugar" Jones, manager of the club, for coming in, but said that headquarters was "pushing" him, and that therefore he had to inspect it. Jones told her, she said, that in his opinion the only time when they had to worry was when Wilstack was off duty; things would be OK while he was on.

Alice asked Guest to bring to bear whatever influence he could to prevent further bothering of her men. Meanwhile Percy hurried back to town and met two detectives at the railroad station to get the lay of the land. These detectives told Harris that some of his men had been getting too bold and advised him to see to it that they handled the business more circumspectly.

The Harrises had another close friend in court—he was Herbert Johnson, Deputy Clerk of Court of Special Sessions (police court). The SIC's report says that Johnson and his wife were both numbers writers for the Harris syndicate. After talking to Harris, Johnson made immediate arrangements on behalf of the prisoners to have bail bonds posted, and paid for them with money given to him by Percy Harris, so that the men would be out of police hands as promptly as possible. Harris left standing instructions with Johnson to make bail immediately for any of his men who were arrested. At the SIC's hearings the counsel asked Johnson why Harris wanted this:

Q. Did he tell you why he wanted them gotten out of jail readily?
A. Well, I guess he said that, he didn't tell me this personally, but I assumed from what he meant that he didn't want them to discuss his business or talk.
Q. Get them out before they could talk; is that it?
A. Yes.
Q. Did Percy Harris give you any money at that time for yourself?
A. Well, Percy Harris said, "Well, here is some money and take it home and give it to the wife and the kids."
Q. How much money did he give you?
A. I think it was fifty dollars.

After getting the men bailed, Johnson got a lawyer for them, and, when they were found guilty, paid their fines and their legal fees out of money given to him for the purpose by Percy Harris. The clerk did not file certificates of conviction against them; during the nine years that he had held his position, he had never filed certificates of conviction in gambling cases unless a jail sentence was imposed. In such a case it was not possible to avoid filing the certificate because it was required before the person could be sent to jail. There was only one such jail sentence meted out in a gambling case during his entire nine years as clerk.

The incident apparently made some of Harris' numbers writers nervous, but Harris was reassuring. He told one of them that, with the exception of the two maverick officers who had made the arrests, the rest of the force was all right. And, as for those two, he said grimly that "they could take orders like anyone else."

Harris, however, had made a wrong guess about Detective Peck. Peck promptly arrested another numbers writer, in a situation in which he had a nearly perfect case. He had sent a third party into the premises with marked money, to place a bet with the numbers writer, a woman named Anna Vassiliades. After she had accepted the money and written down the bet, Peck stepped in, placed her under arrest, and picked up as evidence the marked money and a record book in which the woman jotted down the bets of many customers. She had been conducting the business in a meat market owned by her brother-in-law, James Lemonides.

The SIC's report says that the day after the arrest Detective Peck was asked to report to the office of Assistant District Attorney Anthony Langan. Langan was assigned to prosecute cases for the city in the police court, and had an office in police headquarters. He would be the prosecuting attorney in the airtight case against Mrs. Vassiliades that Detective Peck had brought in.

According to the report, when Peck walked into Langan's office he found three persons waiting for him. One was Langan. The second was Mrs. Vassiliades' lawyer. The third was a man named Benjamin Gingold. Gingold held two city offices: he was city assessment commissioner and he was also a hearing officer assigned to the police court.

His specific function was to preside over departmental trials of police officers. He was, in other words, the man that Peck would have to face, and the man who would decide his fate, if he ever "got in trouble" on his job.

In addition to these two public functions, Gingold was also an attorney in private practice. Although nobody at this conference saw fit to mention it to Peck, Gingold was at this time serving as lawyer for James Lemonides, the man on whose premises Peck had arrested the numbers writer Mrs. Vassiliades. Neither did anyone at the conference tell Peck that, just prior to his being summoned, Gingold had had a long private conference with Assistant DA Langan. The case, of course, was not against Gingold's client, Lemonides. But if Peck's arrest of Mrs. Vassiliades should result in a conviction—and there was every reason to believe that it would if Langan prosecuted it—then Lemonides would in turn be vulnerable to prosecution for knowingly maintaining a premises in which gambling took place.

Not surprisingly, the testimony of Langan and Gingold before the commission do not agree on what was said at their private conference. But its upshot was clear. Langan said that he was willing not to prosecute the case against Mrs. Vassiliades. The problem now was to get Peck to agree, if at all possible.

Peck, then, knew nothing of this. All he knew was that when he stepped into the office he was confronted with Assistant DA Langan, Departmental Hearing Officer Gingold, and Mrs. Vassiliades' lawyer.

Gingold led off. According to Peck, Gingold said that "due to the circumstances he wanted to come down here and talk to me about it [his arrest of Mrs. Vassiliades] and see if something couldn't be done."

The detective was angered when he saw what was in the

wind, but was also nonplussed and didn't know quite what to do. The men facing him were a formidable array.

"The evidence is about as good as you could get," he told them. "A marked bill—found the evidence on the scene, a marked bill, the notebook with the bet registered. And you can't get it much better."

Then Langan stepped in directly. Peck described it to the state investigators at the SIC's public hearings:

Q. Did Mr. Langan say anything at this point?
A. Yes, sir.
Q. Will you tell us what he said?
A. Well, Mr. Langan asked me if it would be all right if we dropped the charges.
Q. How did you answer him?
A. Well, I told him I didn't want to. No.

Gingold and Langan urged him to agree. Peck courageously refused. Finally, says Peck, Langan "asked me if I would feel better if I went to talk to Chief Kelly about it." Relieved, Peck agreed. "I felt that when I went to the chief he would back me," Peck told the commission. He was, however, in for a rude shock. The group of four men walked into the office of Syracuse Police Chief Harold F. Kelly. Langan explained the case to the chief, said he felt there might be extenuating circumstances in this instance, and urged that the case be dropped. Kelly did nothing to defend Peck. "I asked the chief what I should do," said Peck. "I felt I had a good case. And he said, 'You arrested her, it's up to you.'"

Peck saw that he was alone. But he still couldn't bring himself to agree to what was being asked of him. He told the chief that he didn't think the case should be dropped.

That was the last said to him about the matter by any

of the officials involved. A few days later Peck read a big story in the morning papers about the case. It described the arrest, and said that the district attorney's office had decided to drop the case because of insufficient evidence. The story reflected adversely on Peck, as an officer who had made an arrest that couldn't be made to stick. Peck had been thrown to the wolves. Gingold's purpose had been achieved.

"Did Gingold ever tell you that he was representing the man, Mr. James Lemonides?" asked the SIC's counsel. "No sir," said Peck.

Summoned to the public hearings, Langan admitted that Peck had turned over to him for prosecution an airtight case against Mrs. Vassiliades. He saw nothing wrong with Gingold's intervention to protect a client who was not involved in the case to be prosecuted:

Q. Did he [Gingold] ever suggest to you that you didn't have a strong case?
A. Oh, no, no.
Q. He agreed that you had a strong case?
A. Yes, sir.
Q. Yet he asked you to drop it?
A. Yes. Sure.
Q. Did you drop it?
A. I did . . .

Commissioner Myles Lane bore down hard on Langan:

Q. If she had been found guilty, or pleaded, she then might have been in a position to give testimony against Lemonides. You see, this man Gingold was in pleading, telling you in effect that Lemonides was the guilty person.
A. That's right.

Q. By dismissing that case you lost all opportunity of getting a conviction against Lemonides.

A. Except that he stated that the man was just so upset over this happening, it being, you know, a sister-in-law getting in trouble, that he would never do it again. . . . The police felt that it was good law enforcement.

Langan gave some indication that Peck's stubbornness about the matter came to him as a surprise. "All the arresting officers said, whenever these situations arose, they had no objection if a case wasn't made," he explained.

As for Peck, all he had accomplished by his stubbornness was to create a blot on his professional police record and to make himself a marked man. An instructive lesson for anyone tempted to do things his own way instead of "going along" when asked.

The SIC's report states that gamblers in Syracuse received other kinds of help from the police. Since it is an open invitation to trouble for a police force to conduct no antigambling activity whatever in a town where gambling is well known to be rife, "raids" were occasionally conducted. But in some instances the gambling establishments that were about to receive police attention were tipped off.

A patrolman who was a switchboard dispatcher told state investigators that there was an "obvious pattern" of tip-offs by members of the detective division and by certain police higher-ups. Complaints of gambling and vice violations received by the dispatcher were transferred to the detective bureau. Immediately after the detective bureau had received the information, an inside call would be made from the detective bureau to the deputy chief of police. Following this conversation, both parties would hang up and then one or the other would promptly request an outside line. "This would generally be following the complaints received on certain locations, certain establishments," the dispatcher testified. If police were dispatched, the call dispatching them would invariably be made *after* this outside call had been completed. The dispatcher observed that whenever this series of events took place, the raid would fall flat on its face. The cops, entering the suspected premises, would discover no sign of gambling or illegal activity.

A patrolman described a typical experience to the commission. Observing a group of ten men engaged in an illegal card game in a premises called Tops Restaurant, he called the dispatcher from the radio in his car and asked for assistance to make a raid. When a carful of additional men arrived they raided the premises. But the cards, the gambling paraphernalia, and all the evidence were gone. The ten men who had been engaged in the game when the patrolman first peeked in were now standing up with their hands in their pockets, apparently waiting for the police. Shortly afterward the patrolman learned from the dispatcher that immediately after his call for assistance had been relayed to the detective division an outgoing call was made from the detective division to the owner of Tops Restaurant.

Such police cooperation had its price. Levotion "LB" Bell is described in the SIC's report as a "former operator of two houses of prostitution and an after-hours club where illegal gambling took place." The gambling establishment was called the East Side Social Club. Shortly after he opened the club in 1957 he was introduced to Syracuse gambler Nick Rowe. Rowe promised to arrange for police protection for Bell's enterprises in exchange for weekly payments ranging from $125 to $150.

The report states that Bell began to make the payments and found that he was getting his money's worth. On two occasions he received advance warnings from the police just before they made raids, giving him time to remove all evidence of law violation before the raiders arrived. On another occasion a detective began parking his car outside one of Bell's houses of prostitution and making observations of activity. Bell complained to Rowe, and Rowe said that he would talk to the detective. The surveillance immediately ceased. Bell also made direct payments to five Syracuse detectives; one of them received a payment every week.

Another man who wanted to open an after-hours club in Syracuse talked to Nick Rowe about the matter of running such a club without police interference. Rowe consulted with his contacts, says the SIC's report, and a few days later reported that the man could go ahead and open his club if he would make payments of $30 a week. Like Bell, this man found that he was getting his money's worth. At one time the club was visited by a detective in response to a citizen's complaint. The detective arrived while liquor was being sold and served to a roomful of customers after legal hours. The detective grinned and asked the owner if he was selling liquor or "having a private party." The owner, who could not very well deny it, replied that he was selling the liquor. At the public hearings the owner described what happened:

Q. You told him you were running an after-hours club?
A. Yes.
Q. Selling liquor?
A. Yes.
Q. What, if anything, did he then do?
A. He called down [to headquarters] and made a report that I was having a private party.

Alice Harris' brother, Gerald "Buster" Mordecai, is described in the SIC's report as comptroller of the Harris gambling enterprises since 1946. He admitted to commission agents that he annually distributed "Christmas envelopes" to certain parties in the city, including police officers. He was never arrested by the Syracuse police. Another gambler paid off in liquor. Some of the cops were apparently greedy, and he therefore made each one sign a list upon receipt of his gift to avoid double allotments.

Gift giving was so much an accepted part of the system that officers, instead of waiting for the gifts to come to them, engaged in veritable campaigns, soliciting gifts to which they began to feel entitled. Some crooks and criminals were reluctant, but police surveillance of them showed that the force was not entirely without skills where they chose to employ them. "There used to be a joke between us," said one policeman to the commission, describing the police's relationship to an apparently stingy gambler. "He used to try to avoid us every Christmas, and it was a kind of tag game that we were playing." It was a game that the gambler never won.

At Christmastime the word would be passed around headquarters when gifts from underworld sources were ready to be collected. One detective described at the SIC's hearings how it worked:

Q. Tell us how this came about.
A. Well, this was, from my experience and my knowledge, around Christmastime. This would come when the word somehow would be passed through the headquarters, not necessarily the detective office, this went to all branches, where a certain place, that if you stopped by so and so, he would have a bottle or an envelope . . . .
Q. When you say all areas—

A. I mean traffic, motor vehicle, uniformed patrol, detective, youth bureau—all areas.

Q. Vice squad?

A. Yes . . . .

Q. I am concerned with the places which were suspected of illegal activities, that is, criminals passing out money and passing out gifts to police officers. Were these also included among those about which the word was passed around.

A. I don't have first hand knowledge as to whether or not these men are criminals or were convicted, at the time; they were suspected of gambling.

Q. That is what I am talking about: suspected premises, people who were suspected of illegal gambling and criminal activities. Were they also included in the general word that was being passed around at police headquarters?

A. Yes.

At the commission's public hearings Sergeant Thomas Sardino described a raid that he conducted at the Onondaga Square Club, owned by Percy Harris. At 3:15 A.M. Sardino and his cruising partner noticed a large crowd in the premises and many cars parked nearby. It was after legal liquor hours. Sardino radioed for assistance to make a raid, and several other cops arrived. This time there was apparently no tip-off—conceivably because of the early hour, when the top brass of the department was in bed asleep.

Sardino, leading the men into the club, found about twenty people engaged in a dice game. Sardino lined them up and searched them. In the inner breast pocket of Sugar Jones, operator of the establishment and close associate of Percy Harris, Sardino and Mosher found fourteen envelopes. Six of them contained twenty-dollar bills. A name was written in the upper-left-hand corner of each of these envelopes. All six names were identical to the surnames of men then holding the rank of sergeant in the Syracuse Police Department. The remaining eight envelopes, each containing a five-dollar bill, had no writing on the outside.

"What are these?" Sardino asked. "Gifts for the boys," Jones replied. Sardino and Mosher showed the envelopes to the other members of the raiding party, who later corroborated Sardino's account of the event to the commission. The envelopes and money were then returned to Jones.

In reporting on the raid, Sardino and Mosher described the discovery of the envelopes orally to their superiors but did not mention it in their written report. The reasons, obvious enough, were emphasized by the frank statement given to the commission in private hearings by one of Sardino's and Mosher's superior officers: He thought it likely that the two would have been reprimanded for "digging into dirt," and that reprisals against them might well have ensued.

At public hearings Alice Harris testified that Jones told her about the raid and the discovery of the money, but her memory failed her when it came to the names of the police officers who were to be paid off:

Q. Mrs. Harris, Sugar [Jones] told you about this, didn't he?
A. He did.
Q. Did he tell you what police officers that money was intended for?
A. He may have.
Q. Which police officers?
A. I couldn't recall. If I can recall the names, if I can recall it, I will—

The day after Sergeant Sardino testified, his wife, a stenographer in the district attorney's office, received a telephoned murder threat against her husband. It was not carried out.

When conscientious police work did not get a man into active trouble on the Syracuse force, it was likely to be ignored or buried. During the course of his routine police duties, Patrolman James Longo began to receive bits of information and evidence concerning importation of narcotics into the city. The SIC's report states that he went to his superior officer, Captain William McCarthy, and asked for permission to follow up the leads, offering to do the investigative work on his own time if necessary. Permission was granted. Patrolman Longo plunged into the task energetically, and after a substantial investigation he typed a four-page summary report, put it in a sealed envelope, and forwarded it directly to Police Chief Kelly. He described the report at the December 1962 state hearings:

Q. Sergeant Longo, this is a 4-page report, is it not?
A. Yes.
Q. I have added up the total number of persons reported on here and I come to a figure of 40. Does that sound correct to you?
A. Yes, sir, it does.
Q. Does that include not only users of narcotics, but suspect pushers of narcotics?
A. Yes, sir, it does.
Q. Did you indicate in the report the manner of operation of these narcotic dealers?
A. Yes, I did.
Q. Did you identify them by name and address?
A. Yes, sir, I did.

Q. Did you indicate, too, how the narcotics came into Syracuse, from what other cities?

A. Yes, sir, I did.

Q. Did you indicate other cities such as New York City?

A. Yes.

Q. Rochester?

A. Yes.

Q. Buffalo?

A. Yes, sir.

Q. And others?

A. Yes, sir, I did . . .

Q. Was this information which in your judgment required follow-up action?

A. Yes, sir.

Q. Did you see any evidence of this follow-up action?

A. No, sir, I didn't.

Longo heard nothing from Chief Kelly or from anyone else—not even an acknowledgment that the report had been received. After waiting for several months, he asked one of the vice squad members if the report had been received and if any action was going to be taken. The vice squad member simply said that "they had that information before." Other young officers who knew of Longo's work and report asked him about the results, and he told them that it had been dropped into an apparent well of silence. "They were a little disgusted," Longo recalls. "Many times they said, 'If this is the kind of recognition you will get for this kind of work, there is no need to do any more.' "

Longo nevertheless submitted a supplementary report on some of the persons mentioned in his original report. In due time the excellence and accuracy of Longo's work, and the potential for a law-enforcement triumph that it placed in the hands of the Syracuse police, became all too apparent. The SIC's report states that many of the persons that he named have since been arrested for narcotics crimes or crimes related to narcotics. However, every one of the arrests has been made by outside law-enforcement agencies such as the New York State Police or the New York State Bureau of Narcotics. Nothing was done by the vice squad or detective division of the Syracuse police to verify the information contained in the report, to conduct investigations, or to make arrests.

Such an atmosphere in a police department is not created overnight. The lethargy builds slowly over a period of many years, and decay and erosion are usually furthered by progressively bold inroads of ever-expanding criminal activities. Cities whose police forces have moved down this path pay a heavy price. Successive scandals, newspaper exposures, and investigations take place, but in many cases these are insufficient to bring a lasting reversal of the trend. The road back is a long and hard one; civic interest rapidly wanes; criminal elements, which retreat when the lid blows off in periodic scandals, edge in again, slowly but remorselessly, when things quiet down.

So it has been with Syracuse. Percy Harris came to town in 1931, set up his gambling operation on a modest scale, and began making tentative contacts with the police. Within a few years, says the SIC's report, he was kingpin of a gambling syndicate based in Syracuse and operating in other cities, including Fulton, Oswego, Ithaca, Rome, Cortland, and Utica. In 1937 he bought the Onondaga Club in Syracuse, and subsequently bought into other enterprises including two New York City nightclubs.

Police cooperation was a necessary part of every expansion of his illegal areas of activity. He sought it and got it, expanding and consolidating his beachhead at police headquarters with every enlargement of his gambling syndicate. Such arrangements, corrupt in themselves, drain the spirit and vitality from all areas of a police force's work, leaving cynicism and lethargy.

By 1943 there was general awareness in the city that law enforcement was bankrupt. The famous United States police expert, August Vollmer, was brought to the city to study the department. He made the study and submitted a detailed report. For the most part, says SIC, it was filed and forgotten.

Things were simmering again by 1947; a grand jury was summoned to look into gambling. It returned no indictments but sharply criticized the community for its complacency. It also shook its finger at the police:

The evidence does show that there has been a complete lack of police work in respect to gambling. For that, the department of police is entitled to criticism and censure. Out of this investigation should come a resolution on the part of the Chief of Police and the entire department to never again let gambling get started. It can be kept out, and we recommend that unless it is kept out, there should be a clean-up of the department.

Foreman of this grand jury was Anthony A. Henninger. He served as mayor of Syracuse from 1958 to 1962, during which time most of the abuses cited in this chapter took place.

After the grand jury made its report, things quieted down again and remained relatively quiet until 1957, when U.S. Treasury agents raided some gambling premises in Syracuse. Newspapers in the city began to hammer away at the gambling issue and to put editorial pressure on the police.

In 1959 there was another grand jury investigation. In June, 1959, the jury, in its report, stated, "Gambling is not a major problem in the city." Four months later, on

October 23, the State Investigation Commission and the New York State Police made a series of simultaneous gambling raids and arrests in Syracuse in connection with the commission's investigation of gambling in central and western New York State.

At public hearings on syndicated gambling held by the State Investigation Commission in April 1960 in New York City, it was shown that bookmakers in Syracuse were doing business with gamblers in fourteen cities in eleven states, in the District of Columbia, and in Canada.

On May 13, 1960, the commission and the criminal intelligence unit of the New York State Police struck directly at the Percy Harris empire, in a series of raids that ultimately resulted in convictions and brief jail terms for the Harrises.

Again, the newspapers were up in arms. In its May 15, 1960, issue the Syracuse *Post-Standard* said:

This kind of widespread racket does not continue in any community year after year without the tacit knowledge and consent of prosecutors and others charged with law enforcement. It is not logical to assume that a few outside investigators can spend a few days in any city and uncover illegal activities not previously known of by local authorities.

On the same day the Syracuse *Herald-Journal* called for action:

The lack of direction of the Syracuse Police Department has reached the point where it can be only described as pathetic. A COMPLETE REORGANIZATION IS URGENTLY NEEDED, STARTING FROM THE TOP.

Mayor Henninger promised action. "Recent developments have proved embarrassing to me and I am completely out of patience," he told the press. "I have seriously studied the situation and in the very near future, I will announce certain reorganization plans for the Police Department."

In July 1960 the mayor appointed Charles F. Sloane as special police administrator to "reorganize and rejuvenate" the department. Sloane left the job after seventeen months, charging the mayor with interference and with ignoring his recommendations.

Once again the lid blew off when the State Investigation Commission conducted its six days of public hearings in December 1962. Chief Kelly resigned after the third day of the hearings, and Samuel Hyneman, who had moved up from captain of detectives to first deputy chief of the force, resigned the next day.

In January 1963 a sobered city chose a new police chief, Patrick V. Murphy, and a new first deputy, William H. T. Smith, both former members of the New York City Police Department with impressive qualifications. They immediately plunged into their Herculean task—to find and chart the road back. On February 27, Chief Murphy announced a complete reorganization of the detective division. Soon thereafter he and Smith established a criminal intelligence unit.

But reform is a hard job—how hard, only dedicated reformers like Murphy and Smith, who must stay at the task after public interest has died away, can know. On March 19, 1964, *The New York Times* reported that ninety men had been seized by state police in upstate New York gambling raids. The raided establishments had been doing a total annual gross business of $25 million. The raids took place in a number of places, but the biggest killings had been made in the Buffalo area and in Rochester, Albany —and Syracuse.

CHAPTER SIX

Police Corruption in Suburbia

For a full week in October 1963 ranking officers of police departments in New York's fashionable Westchester County alternated with gamblers in parading reluctantly across the State Investigation Commission's witness stand. It was hard to tell who had the shorter memory, the gamblers or the cops. But the combined memory problems of six police forces in Westchester County could not prevent the hearings from putting a vivid spotlight on a new trend in American crime. Syndicate leaders, like other successful businessmen, have been moving to the suburbs. In one sense their motives are the same as those of any suburbanite —they are seeking peace and quiet. But the peaceful atmosphere that they seek—and find—in prosperous suburban towns, is the bliss of ineffective small-town law enforcement.

In many of the nation's big cities, increasing police sophistication and increasingly effective methods for dealing with crime syndicates have made things uncomfortable for criminals accustomed to relatively easy evasion of the law. But the suburbs are something else again. Police forces are small, their facilities are limited, and their authority stops at the town line. A syndicate that moves into the suburbs can set up a coordinated network of activity in a number of suburban cities and towns. Such a syndicate is often numerically bigger than the police forces in the towns in which it operates. A syndicate member who finds himself in trouble with a town's police force can simply get in his car and drive a mile or so to remove himself from police jurisdiction. If a town clamps down on a syndicate operation, little is lost; the operation can be suspended in that town until things quiet down, and the rest of the operation in other towns is unaffected. Coordinated efforts among the myriad police forces of suburbia to wipe out a well-organized syndicate would be difficult or impossible to achieve, even if the facilities, the community interest, and the will were present.

The typical commuting resident of the "bedroom suburbs" surrounding the nation's great metropolises is a split personality, and the suburban town in which he resides usually gets the short end of the split. His work, his interests, his spiritual identity are with the city; he is a cosmopolite, not a "small-towner" at heart. He has moved to the suburbs to get a little grass and some good schools for his children; when they grow up and leave home, he is quite likely to move back to the city again.

The two big things that a suburban commuter usually wants from the police force of the town in which he lives are protection of his property from burglars and protection of his daughters from sexual assault. He sometimes hopes or expects that the police will overlook small law infractions of which he may be guilty, and law infractions, small or not so small, of which his children may be guilty. Numerous recent cases show that he is not above bringing substantial pressure to achieve the latter end.

The cosmopolitan intellectual living in the suburbs also brings the powerful solvent of his ideas to bear on local law-enforcement problems. There is a strong tendency among intellectuals to assume that police are corrupt, stupid public servants. Everyone has an inventory of horrifying or hilarious police stories to exchange at parties. In addition, many intellectuals have a hard time taking certain "crimes" seriously. High on the list of "intellectually OK" crimes are gambling and, sometimes, prostitution. Many feel, secretly or not too secretly, that both fulfill ageless human needs, that they will go on whatever the laws say, and that efforts to suppress them are at best silly, at worst genuinely wrong.

Two *New York Times* reporters sampled public opinion in Westchester County after the State Investigation Commission's hearing had shown that local police had become pawns in the hands of immense gambling syndicates. Reporter McCandlish Phillips noted a statement made by a commission spokesman after the hearings: "We're giving them [Westchester County residents] the facts. Now we're giving them the ball." However, said Phillips, Westchesterites "don't seem to care much about 'the facts' and thus show no disposition to take 'the ball.' . . . A common reaction is that gambling is an elemental human urge and that there is no use trying to stop it. What is the harm of a person's stopping in at a stationery store and placing a small bet as a diversion?" Homer Bigart wrote from White Plains on October 22, "Charges of gambling and police venality provoke nothing but yawns in this sector of suburbia." One commuter told him that the whole subject of police corruption was taboo as far as the commuters were concerned. "We have to stay friendly with the cops," the commuter said. "Whenever we throw a big party we need a cop to tell guests where to park. Last time we even used one as a bartender. It was legitimate moonlighting."

Under the circumstances, police incentive to strain their meager facilities to the limit and to step on all kinds of toes to give the community a kind of law enforcement in which it has no interest has been nil. Local police are wise connoisseurs of power structures, and sensitive barometers of community mood. In suburban towns people want pleasant personal relationships, and peace.

Another group of power-structure connoisseurs are the heads of gambling and crime syndicates. It did not take them long to perceive the situation in the new suburbia. They have moved in.

Westchester County is one of the wealthiest and most beautiful commuting suburban areas in the nation. Lying immediately north of the Bronx boundary of New York City, the county comprises 435 square miles and had a population of 808,891 at the time of the 1960 census. Within its borders lie six cities, eighteen towns, and twenty-two villages. Law enforcement is primarily the responsibility of local police. There are thirty-nine city, town, and village police departments in the county. Six of the forces are moderately large—the Yonkers force has 342 men; New Rochelle, 154; White Plains, 154; Mount Vernon, 178; Port Chester, 55. Most of the rest consist of a handful of men. Each department is autonomous; there is little coordinated activity.

In November 1960 a rookie patrolman on the New Rochelle police force wrote a secret letter to the State Investigation Commission, which at that time was conducting its study of organized gambling in central and western New York State. "This city," said the rookie, "is overrun with gamblers." He suggested that the commission conduct an investigation—"without the aid of the New Rochelle Police Department."

It was not the first letter that the commission had received from Westchester County. A detailed letter from a resident of Mount Vernon listed locations "where bookies, numbers takers and similar cheap rackets are openly and knowingly operated with police protection and guidance." Two of the locations were near police headquarters. A mother in Yonkers wrote that policy operators were hanging around the city's public schools, taking bets from schoolchildren during lunch hours. Swarms of children, including her own son, were using their lunch money to play the exciting game. She had filed a complaint with the Yonkers police, but they seemed bored, and nothing had happened.

In 1961 and 1962 commission agents went to Westchester County and, with no trouble, placed bets on horses and numbers at 218 different locations in sixteen communities. "With but one or two exceptions," says the commission's report, "all of the places were stores of various types, open to the street and general public. Most were located on busy thoroughfares and presumably subject to constant police patrol and scrutiny." Some were "stationery stores," furnished with dusty showcases and shelves and containing only token stock. "Dry-cleaning establishments" had no clothes on their racks, but were visited by scores of persons each day, none of whom carried clothes to or from the premises. In "shoe repair shops," machinery was rusty from lack of use. A commission agent entered one of these places and asked the man behind the counter to fix his shoes. "Are you kidding?" the man asked.

At one "stationery store" three numbers writers were working full time taking bets over the open counter, with as many as twelve people at a time waiting in line to place their bets. "Next!" the writers would shout briskly as each customer was taken care of.

Evidence of active police assistance came directly from the experiences of the commission agents while placing their bets. One agent entered a gambling premises run by a well-known major bookmaker and numbers operator, Anthony "Teddy Bear" Calise, at 20 New Street, Yonkers. The premises, a candy and cigar store, was a regular hangout for many members of the Yonkers police force, and cops often called it the Fifth Precinct. Before accepting the agent's bet Calise said, "Wait a moment," left the store, crossed the street, and entered another store where a Yonkers police officer was standing near the window looking the agent over. Calise spoke briefly to the officer, then returned to accept the bet. The agent pretended to be angry. "You're trying to set me up," he growled, meaning that Calise was "giving him away" to the cops. Not so, Calise explained; he was just checking to see if the cop knew him as a federal agent. There was nothing to fear from local law-enforcement officers, Calise said. He nodded in the direction of the police officer who was still in the store across the street. "If he walked in right now, nothing would happen," Calise commented soothingly.

The 218 premises at which the agents made bets did not, the commission believed, represent the total of such places in operation; the actual number was apparently substantially higher. "Restrictions in time and manpower prevented the checking of reliable information concerning many others," the commission's report said. From March 1962 to April 1963 the commission conducted a series of raids, arresting seventy-eight persons and seizing numerous records.

A check of the criminal records of twenty-eight higher-ups who had been caught in the commission's net showed an aggregate total of forty-eight prior convictions for crimes including gambling, narcotics traffic, burglary, extortion, robbery, and rape. The seized documents revealed that there were seven separate major gambling syndicates in the county. Total business of the syndicates was estimated at $30 million annually, of which $20 million came from bookmaking (largely horse betting) and $10 million from the numbers racket. On bookmaking the syndicates raked off 20 percent, or $4 million a year. From the policy racket the rake-off was 35 percent, or $3.5 million for the "little guys"—the writers and controllers—and 37.5 percent or $3.75 million for the policy bankers and syndicate leaders. A net profit of nearly $8 million a year was therefore available to syndicate heads from gambling in Westchester County.

Where did the money go? Some of it, of course, went to provide the comforts of life to the top men. But there was plenty left over. Some, the commission found, went into vast pools of capital for loan-sharking. Loan-sharks make money available to desperate people, some of them gamblers and underworld figures, some of them legitimate citizens, at interest rates that usually run about 100 percent in eight weeks. The rates are enforced by syndicate terrorists, who threaten the persons and families of those unwilling or unable to repay, and who carry out their threats when the syndicate thinks it necessary. Another portion of the funds was being used to put muscle into one of the expanding activities of modern crime syndicates—entrance into selected areas of legitimate commerce. Quarters handed to newsstand numbers writers by Westchester commuters were financing incursion of syndicates into unions, the jukebox industry, and the restaurant and entertainment business.

Other bits and pieces of evidence scattered throughout the seized records pointed to underworld relationships with prominent personalities in mysterious activities spreading across the nation. Among the documents seized at the home of syndicate bookmaker Michael Yannicelli, a previously convicted gambler, was a United States Trotting Association ownership registration certificate for the horse First Flyer. The certificate was not made out to Yannicelli; it showed the owner of the horse to be movie star Scott Brady. Records showed that the purchase price of the horse had been paid by Yannicelli, along with all training, feeding, and boarding bills. The commission sent an invitation to Brady at his home to come to New York and explain what the arrangement was about. Brady declined to appear before the commission.

Westchester gamblers and police officers did not have Brady's option of refusing to appear. In the October 1963 hearings they provided, unwillingly, the basic picture of a wealthy community living with crime.

Peace is the key. A certain power apparatus appears on the scene—the gambling syndicate. It has certain obvious areas of strength, including its intercity and intertown network of operation, and its involvement in an activity to which the public is morally indifferent. These areas of strength correspond to the local police force's areas of greatest weakness. To assault this enemy with the available apparatus would involve immense effort with very dubious prospects of success. There is an alternative. One can live with it; one can have a tacit understanding that will bring relaxation and peace on both sides, and in the community. Big-city forces often make this decision, in circumstances in which the strength and resources of the police are much more a match for the gamblers if the cops choose to fight. In Westchester the decision of local police forces to acknowledge the enemy's power could hardly be called surprising.

Living with a syndicate does not imply constant contact

with it so much as the observance of certain boundaries and ground rules by both sides and an acknowledgment of certain areas of common interest. The gamblers understand that the police cannot completely ignore gambling. Police must maintain lists of suspected premises, must "inspect" them, and must sometimes make arrests. The police, for their part, usually find "nothing suspicious" when they make their "inspections" of such premises; make arrests infrequently; and, when they do make arrests, pick on the little guys and leave the big guys alone.

Gamblers must understand that their behavior must be reasonably circumspect. If they will do their part by maintaining low visibility, that makes it easier for the police to play their end of the game by maintaining that a reasonable level of police efficiency has revealed little or no illegal activity.

Direct contact is sometimes necessary. Individual police officers often expect a little "taste" of the millions of dollars that the syndicate is able to rake in as a result of the agreement. Police must sometimes have a talk with a gambler who is not being discreet, or whose premises are too near the precinct station. In touchy situations, police will tip off gamblers of forthcoming raids. Gamblers, for their part, will often have a quiet talk with police before starting up operations in a new location or a new area.

Each side is in a position to do certain kinds of favors for the other. The police can help a syndicate head to keep his men in line by threatening to harass and arrest men who do not take the gang leader's orders. Syndicate heads and gang leaders, for their part, can often help policemen to get promotions; their personal acquaintance and influence with civic and political leaders are usually greater than that of the average policeman, and they are sometimes in a position to bargain for favors on a police-man's behalf.

As with all clandestine "arrangements," the smooth operation of such an agreement can occasionally be threatened by an untoward or embarrassing incident. Most common is the rookie cop or maverick detective who makes a raid or arrest that isn't in the agreement. Police and gamblers play such situations by ear. They can be dangerous, especially if the rookie or maverick is stubborn and the arrested man has been caught with some evidence that incriminates both sides. A way is usually found to negotiate these shoal waters, although once in a while such an incident can topple a police-protected crime empire.

Despite many contradictions in testimony there was evidence that events in Westchester followed every phase of the classic pattern. The atmosphere of defeat and cynicism engendered among the police by the "agreement" also did its share to produce some uniquely bizarre happenings.

The SIC's report says that on May 4, 1960, the sheriff of Westchester County passed on to New Rochelle Chief of Police Edward McCaffrey a citizen's complaint about gambling. The complaint stated that Peter Rispole's candy store in New Rochelle was a busy numbers-writing establishment. McCaffrey passed the complaint on to the vice squad. Detective James C. Link of the squad went to Rispole's store and arrested him. He was convicted and fined $300.

Soon thereafter Rispole met Link and complained about the arrest. "What was his explanation?" the SIC asked Rispole. "He said, 'Pete, we had to pinch you. We were told to come out and pinch you.' That is the time they found evidence in my garbage can, torn up slips of paper," Rispole replied. The SIC says that the two men talked over the problem, and agreed on a warning signal that Link would use to tip off Rispole in the future when things were getting hot. The signal was "cloudy weather."

Late that year things started to warm up again, and on November 3 the vice squad sent an undercover man to Rispole's store to look it over. The day before, Link phoned Rispole and suggested that he "take a vacation" on November 3. "It looks like cloudy weather," said forecaster Link. When the undercover man arrived he found no evidence of gambling on the premises.

When he took the stand at the public hearings Link solemnly denied ever making advance-warning arrangements with Rispole. At the private hearings Link had taken a different tack; he found himself suffering from acute memory paralysis. The dialogue, typical of what the commission encountered repeatedly in its investigation, is worth quoting in full:

Q. Before we had this off the record discussion, Mr. Link, I asked you certain questions. Let me ask you this now so that there is no question in your mind: Have you ever given any information to a gambler or a suspect gambler about police activity; about an inspection that was going to take place; about a raid that was going to take place; about the fact that the police were going to visit the suspect gambler's place, or anything along those lines?

A. To my recollection I did not. As I say, I have to think about it.

Q. I don't understand what you have to think—

A. I can't answer yes or no. I—

Q. You understand the question, don't you?

A. I understand the question, but my mind is confused now.

I'd have to think, to recall if I did or not. As it stands now, I don't recall any time.

Q. You don't recall whether you did or not?

A. I don't recall.

Q. You understand the question: it is a simple one; isn't it?

A. I don't recall if I did.

Q. But you understand the question?

A. I understood the question.

Q. You want an opportunity to have your memory refreshed: is that it?

A. Yes.

Q. Let me give it to you. I will ask you about a specific gambler and that will refresh your recollection. Do you know Peter Rispole?

A. I know Pete. I locked him up a couple of times.

Q. Have you ever given him advance knowledge about police activity?

A. I might have gone in the place and told him to be careful, if he gets caught he gets caught. That is the best of my recollection.

Q. Did you ever tell him that it might be a good idea for him not to be around the next day?

A. I couldn't recall that.

Q. Do you deny that you ever gave him advice to be away from his place the following day?

A. I wouldn't put it that way. As I said, if we made an inspection I might have told him "Look. Be careful. If you get caught you will get caught." That is the best I can—

Q. You mean, before the inspection you told him to be careful?

A. No. I wouldn't say before.

Q. I am asking you if you ever told him before an inspection to be careful or to take a vacation?

A. I don't recall.

Q. You don't recall?

A. I don't recall.

Q. I will be a bit more specific. On or about November 2 or 3, 1961, did you contact Peter Rispole at 41 First Street, the Blue Room, and tell him he'd better take a vacation the following day?

A. I don't recall that.

Q. You deny that you did it.

A. I don't recall it.

Q. You don't remember?

A. I don't remember doing that, no, sir.

Q. And then he mentioned your name, "Link," on the telephone and you chewed him out? Do you remember it now?

A. I don't remember it, no, sir.

Q. You don't deny it, do you?

A. I don't deny it, but I don't remember it.

In its 1964 report the commission stated flatly that the warning arrangements were made and that the tip-off was given.

Peter Rispole was an active and successful gambler, but the SIC's report states that there were bigger ones, including syndicate operator Anthony "Chick" D'Amore. Patrolman Frederick Weber of the Mount Vernon force nearly precipitated a classic "embarrassing situation" on the night of November 22, 1960, says the SIC, when he entered the office of a gas station on the corner of Mt. Vernon and Lincoln Avenues. Anthony D'Amore and Anthony "Tony the Pimp" De Fillippo, a low-level flunky in the syndicate, were standing near the counter; D'Amore had a fistful of papers in his hand, which Weber realized were gambling slips.

Weber had caught the kingpin with the goods. He told SIC that he seized D'Amore's wrist and hand with both his own hands, closing D'Amore's fist on the slips of paper. Continuing to hold D'Amore in this way, he led him out

of the station and turned him over, slips in hand, to Detective Nicholas Bianco who was in the car outside. Bianco
took both D'Amore and De Fillippo to police headquarters. There Bianco conferred with Captain Harry Traver,
head of the detectives. Traver instructed Bianco *to release
D'Amore and to book De Fillippo for possession of the
slips.*

Bianco had not seen what had transpired inside the gas
station. At the commission's hearings he contradicted
Weber's testimony that Weber had led D'Amore to the car
with the slips in D'Amore's fist. Weber was carrying the
slips, Bianco said. Regarding D'Amore, Bianco said lamely,
"I thought he was in the hierarchy, where he couldn't be
caught with slips on him. He was too big a man in the
policy racket."

The commission queried Captain Traver on his decision
to release D'Amore:

Q. In other words, you took the word of someone who did not
   see the thing over the man who was present and who caught
   this big gambling man red-handed? Is that right?
A. In this case, yes. Yes.

The SIC's report says that an even bigger fish got away
on March 9, 1962. The Mount Vernon police received
an anonymous tip that the driver of a Tri-Home Beverage
truck had been turning over some kind of package every
day between 2:05 and 2:15 P.M., at the corner of Monroe
Street and Franklin Avenue, to a man who came by in a
car. Captain of Detectives John D. McCaffrey, Lt. James
Rezza, his second in command, Detective Edward Magner,
and Detective Bianco went to the spot. At the appointed
time the truck came along. Instead of waiting for the car
to arrive at the rendezvous, which would have enabled the

police to catch both men in the act with the evidence, Detective Bianco promptly stepped out and arrested the truck driver, one Peter Severino. They then left the scene, taking Severino and his policy slips to the police station before the pick-up car arrived.

Detective Magner was then asked to make out the arrest report, even though Bianco had made the arrest.

At the hearings Detective Magner said that he had been told that the others knew who was driving the passenger car that they didn't wait for. It was Steve Corrado, one of the biggest policy bankers, who was subsequently picked up by the commission in its 1963 raids. He was involved in two syndicates whose annual take, calculated from records seized by the commission, exceeded $3 million.

Q. Who gave you the name of Steve Corrado?

A. Well, it could have been either McCaffrey or Lieutenant Rezza.

Q. Steve Corrado belongs to a family that is fairly well known in the gambling fraternity, isn't that correct?

A. That is correct. . . .

Q. Wasn't it peculiar that they should ask you to sign the report since they knew that Steve Corrado was involved?

A. Possibly.

Q. Do you feel, then, that they requested that you sign this report even though you were not the arresting officer, but perhaps in any future questioning like today, like you might be left holding the bag?

A. Maybe, I wouldn't say for sure.

Q. Now that you look back upon it, do you think—

A. Now that you opened my eyes to it, yes.

Q. Don't you feel that way now?

A. Yes sir, I do.

In Yonkers the police headquarters moved in September

1962 from Wells Avenue to a new location on Columbia Place. This brought the police within the shadow of a numbers-writing operation run by James Conte at 221 Nepperhan Avenue. Conte's operation, run from a stationery store "front," had been on the suspect-premises list for four years. Lieutenant Joseph Nader told the SIC that he had visited the premises many times from 1957 to October 1962. He said that he had never found any evidence of gambling.

With police headquarters moving in next door, Conte's operation was apparently too close for comfort. On October 1 Lieutenant Nader visited Conte. Conte described the visit to the State Investigation Commission:

Q. They told you the new headquarters was there; is that right?
A. Well, I knew they were there.
Q. You couldn't operate any more that close to headquarters; is that right? You had to find a new place?
A. Yes, something to that effect.
Q. Tell me what they told you.
A. They just said to me, "Jimmy, you are no good here."
Q. Did you ask why?
A. No. I didn't have to ask questions like that.

The commission asked Lieutenant Nader why the police had suddenly become so interested in closing down Conte's shop:

Q. If you were going to close him down why wasn't the action taken when police headquarters was on Wells Avenue?
A. Couldn't answer that.
Q. I beg your pardon.
A. I can't answer that.

Conte moved a few doors down the street to 235 Nepper-

han Avenue, setting himself up as a "television tube store."
This removed him, apparently, from the range of embar-
rassment of the Yonkers police. The commission asked
Lieutenant Nader why Conte was able to operate at both
premises over such a long period of time without a single
arrest. "I can't explain it," Lieutenant Nader answered.

According to testimony before the commission the threat
of selective arrest procedures was, on occasion, used to help
syndicate leaders keep their organizations in line. The arrangement was described to the SIC by Frank A. Ciliberti,
former sergeant of detectives of the Yonkers department:

Q. These writers and percentage bookies belong to a particular
syndicate. Is that right?
A. Yes, sir.
Q. And are there occasions when one syndicate will try to grab
a writer or a bookie from another syndicate?
A. Yes, sir.
Q. And/or a writer or a percentage bookie will try to leave one
syndicate and go to another? Is that right?
A. Yes, sir.
Q. This is a source of some possible trouble, is that correct?
A. Yes, sir.
Q. And it creates excitement and disturbance and trouble in
the gambling business, is that correct?
A. That's right.
Q. And that was the kind of thing that the police don't want
to see happening, is that correct?
A. That's right, sir.
Q. Are you saying when you were asked that question, that if
one of these writers or percentage people try to leave his
boss bookmaker, or his boss syndicate, and go to another,
that a police officer would keep him in line or threaten to
keep him in his own syndicate by threatening to lock him
up?

A. That is not necessarily what anybody else might do. That was my own personal opinion.

Q. You said that as a matter of fact. In your experience in the Yonkers Police Department, has that happened?

A. Yes, sir.

Q. It has happened.

A. Yes, sir.

Q. Who, sir, is the police officer engaged in that kind of practice?

A. I don't recall, sir.

Many gamblers in Westchester testified that police arrangements had their price. In New Rochelle a numbers writer named Wilbur Kittle testified that, starting about 1950, he began writing numbers in the office of the taxi service that he operated. Gambler Canio Di Napoli of New Rochelle, whose syndicate operated in both New Rochelle and Yonkers, agreed to handle Kittle's business.

Q. Did Canio say that he would take your policy business in 1950, when you began?

A. That was right.

Q. What did he say with regard to the police department?

A. He said I had nothing to worry about.

Di Napoli told Kittle that in the event of an arrest the syndicate would provide an attorney and bondsmen and would pay all expenses. But Kittle realized that arrest was unlikely. In addition to whatever arrangements Di Napoli had made, Kittle made his own. He told the commission that, about two years after he started his numbers operation, he began making payments himself to the vice squad and other members of the New Rochelle Police Department. He made the payoffs at prearranged times throughout the year, at the North Pelham Railroad Station at night. One of the officers to whom he stated he made payoffs was Detective James Link, the man who had tipped off gambler Peter Rispole by forecasting "stormy weather" the day before the vice squad had checked Rispole's premises. Kittle also testified that he gave cash gifts to policemen at Christmastime and when they went on vacation. He identified seventeen officers of the New Rochelle force besides Link whom he had paid off.*

Although high-ranking officers of the New Rochelle department admitted that Kittle had long been suspected of running a numbers operation, neither his name nor the location of his office appeared on the suspect premises list until he was arrested in a commission raid in March 1962. The SIC's report states that every year policemen came around to Kittle and solicited ads for the *Police Benevolent Association Journal.* They also sold him tickets for the Policemen's Ball. Kittle, along with other gamblers, was happy to contribute.

In Yonkers, numbers writer Louis "Louie the Hat" Angelori testified that he operated a tobacco and candy store on a profit-sharing concession from Teddy Bear Calise, the gambler who had stepped across the street to check with a Yonkers policeman before taking a commission agent's bet. When Calise was not in the store Angelori wrote numbers, accepted horse bets, and sold the store's regular merchandise. Angelori said that this one establishment did about $30,000 a month in bookmaking and numbers business. During the period of his employment he

---

* Thirteen of these eighteen officers denied—under oath at the commission's private hearings or in sworn affidavits—ever receiving money from Kittle. One officer was deceased. Three of the remaining four officers, all of whom were retired, were offered an opportunity to testify at private hearings. They either refused or failed to appear at their scheduled examinations. The commission was unable to locate the remaining retired officer.

stated that he had seen Calise making regular payments to four captains and nine detectives of the Yonkers force (the total strength of the Yonkers detective division was twenty men). As in New Rochelle, the officers swore to the commission that they had never received such payments. But in twenty years of gambling operations in Yonkers, Calise was arrested only four times, and a period of nine years elapsed between his third arrest in 1951 and his last arrest in 1960. The four arrests resulted in aggregate fines of $900 and a total of five days in jail. His operation was never interrupted.

The jovial relationship between the police and Teddy Bear was indicated in Angelori's testimony. Angelori described typical visits by one of the captains who, he stated, was being paid off by Calise:

Q. What did he do when he came in?
A. He cleans the store out.
Q. What do you mean, he cleans the store out?
A. A carton of cigarettes, two cartons of cigarettes. . . .
Q. He does not pay for it?
A. "Put it on the pad." . . .
Q. What else did you see him do?
A. He looks around, makes believe he is looking for bets and slips and then "Where is the boss?" "He ain't here." "Where is he?" "Where is that wop?" He calls him wop . . .
Q. Were there times when Teddy Bear was there, is that right?
A. That's right . . .
Q. What would happen when Teddy Bear was there?
A. He was saying, no business. No business.
Q. Did you hear him talk to Teddy Bear Calise?
A. Yes.
Q. What conversation did you hear?
A. He said, business is tough.
Q. Who would say that?

A. Teddy.

Q. Yes.

A. "Well, what you are saying is business is tough. All the time I come down here, business is always tough." He said, "You have got a Cadillac out there, a six-thousand-dollar Cadillac out there."

In White Plains, shoe repairman Angelo Zuzolo started writing numbers shortly after the Second World War. He said that his business was handled by John and Pat Vercase, who paid him 25 percent of the gross business which he turned in. Zuzolo said that he made payments to a number of members of the White Plains detective division. He also stated that the police would often come in and ask him to buy tickets to various police functions. Zuzolo always gave the police the money but never bothered to take the tickets:

Q. You gave them money but you let them keep the tickets?

A. What I going to do with the ticket?

Zuzolo was arrested four times, on each occasion receiving a nominal fine. The smooth flow of his business was never interrupted.

It is only a short step from police toleration of gambling to active participation by members of the force. The SIC's report says that in New Rochelle several members of the detective division were frequent participants in professional card and dice games run by one of the syndicates. A local businessman told the commission of four different locations in the city where police gambled with syndicate members. One of the premises was Hodges Plumbing Company, conveniently located across the street from police headquarters, where, he said, three detectives and a police sergeant were regular players. The games ran day and night, sometimes lasting until 5 A.M. The police officers were by no means favorite players as far as the gamblers were concerned. A losing officer would often refuse to quit and would "borrow" money from the operator of the game to continue. The operator realized that if the policeman continued to lose he could not expect to get the loan back.

The situation was made known to the highest ranking members of the force. The SIC's report states that on June 2, 1960, New Rochelle Chief of Police Edward McCaffrey received an anonymous complaint which read in part, "I know that you have just locked up a crap game in Hodges Plumbing Shop. From what they tell me your favorite boy Terche, was getting his bid for years. As people seen him go in there, also amount of police officers. As you and I know, they all engaged in that crap game."

The "Terche" in the complaint was Detective Edward Terche of the vice squad. Chief McCaffrey forwarded the complaint to the vice squad for investigation. The investigation was conducted by Detective Edward Terche. He filed a report stating that he could find no evidence of illegal activity.

Police relationships with gamblers can lead to increasingly deep police involvement in crime. Three witnesses said in sworn testimony before the commission that an active participant in card and dice games was New Rochelle Detective Kenneth Hanlan. Hanlan denied it; but he did not deny that he was a partner in Stu's Luncheonette with a man named Stuart Bottnick, and that the two men hired a third, Richard "Duke" Figliuzzi, a man whose criminal record includes two prison terms for narcotics convictions, as their employee at the luncheonette. Stu's Luncheonette was a busy location for taking numbers and horse bets; its business was handled by the syndicate headed by gambler Joe Tufo. No arrest for gambling was ever made at Stu's Luncheonette while Hanlan was a partner. Neither were there ever any formal police inspections, although police officers dropped in for coffee. Hanlan said that he had no idea that his partner and employee were running gambling activities in the eatery, and was at a loss to account for the stories that they told.

Bottnick testified at the public hearing that he and Hanlan divided the gambling profits fifty-fifty each Saturday afternoon, carefully separating this money from the regular luncheonette revenues for which there was a checking account. One day, said Bottnick, Hanlan came in and said that he had swung a good deal. They were going to transfer their gambling business from the syndicate run by Joe Tufo to that run by another chieftain, Jess Harvey. Harvey had paid him $1,500 for the business, and Hanlan split this with Bottnick according to Bottnick's account. However, Bottnick testified, the new business deal brought swift trouble. Tufo's goons paid Bottnick a visit, told him that the "main office" did not like the switch, and warned that "If I didn't turn in to Tufo, I couldn't turn in at all." Hanlan and Bottnick capitulated, according to Bottnick; they gave their business back to Tufo and returned Harvey's money.

Meanwhile, Bottnick related, other things were afoot. Ex-con Figliuzzi, the luncheonette employee, also worked as a cook at another restaurant. He discovered that the owners of this restaurant were using butter stolen from the Daitch-Shopwell food chain. Figliuzzi told Bottnick and Hanlan about it, and brought them some of the stolen butter for use at Stu's Luncheonette. Bottnick and Figliuzzi both testified that they and Hanlan decided to turn this information into money. They would sell the identity of the thief to Daitch-Shopwell and split the proceeds.

They said that Hanlan first wanted to be sure that the butter represented stolen goods. They stated that Figliuzzi and Hanlan broke into the basement of the other restaurant at night and there Hanlan saw the stolen butter in Daitch-Shopwell wrappers. Satisfied, Hanlan approached Shopwell and offered to identify the thief for $1,500. Shopwell agreed; Hanlan identified the thief, and Shopwell paid. Bottnick and Figliuzzi each testified that they had received their shares of $500 each.

Figliuzzi also testified that Hanlan would furnish him with information and leads concerning good potential burglary and robbery victims. One of them, said Figliuzzi, was Joe Tufo, the man who had put his foot down when Hanlan and Bottnick had tried to change syndicates. Figliuzzi cased Tufo's home but decided that there was too much lighting in the area.

Figliuzzi also said at the hearings that he asked Hanlan to get him a gun:

Q. Will you tell us about that?
A. I had something—some piece of work that I was interested in. And I needed something to use to accomplish this.
Q. In other words, you were going to commit a robbery.
A. Yes.

Figliuzzi said that Hanlan got him a .45 Colt revolver, and later a sawed-off .22 rifle. Hanlan denied it.

Now came a new venture—a proposed payroll robbery. Figliuzzi told the SIC that early in 1962 Hanlan had a talk with him about a woman who ate regularly at the luncheonette. Figliuzzi knew her only as a customer, but

Hanlan told him that she worked for a nearby trucking company and walked to the bank every Wednesday morning to pick up the cash payroll. Because Figliuzzi was known to the woman and to others in the neighborhood, it would be necessary to bring a third party in on the scheme. The third party, Hanlan suggested, should be a man named Herbert Martin.

"Hanlan," Figliuzzi said, "had told me about this guy Martin, you know, and he said that Martin was looking for somebody to work with, and he thought that if we could get together, we might be able to come to something. So one night Martin came down and identified himself and he said that Hanlan had sent him. I sort of knew his appearance, his face, you know. But I never had known him."

Figliuzzi said that it was decided that Martin would pull the holdup. Figliuzzi would wait for the woman to leave the trucking company, drive a couple of blocks to a prearranged point, pick up Martin, let him pull the job, then pick him up again and drive away. Hanlan's role was to wait at nearby police headquarters for Figliuzzi's call telling him that the woman had left for the bank. Hanlan would then go to the bank and watch to be sure that the woman had made the withdrawal. If for any reason she hadn't he would give Martin the high sign and wave him off. He would also "cover" while the crime was being committed—a word whose exact meaning was not spelled out in the testimony.

The robbery was set for February 21, 1962. On the preceding day Figliuzzi phoned Martin and told him that he had talked to "Mr. H." who "is going to work with us tomorrow." Figliuzzi was to "lay on the scene until the chick pulls out" and then notify Hanlan who "will move down to the corner, check what she does while she is in there, like we don't draw a blank . . . because she may go in a store or something." Martin agreed and told Figliuzzi that he had his "action" (gun) in readiness.

When the woman left the trucking firm on the morning of February 21 Figliuzzi called Hanlan at police headquarters and asked him to leave the station house.

"Where do you want me to go?" Hanlan asked.

"Well, just to the point, that point on the corner and see what she is doing there."

"OK, I will cover you . . . bye," said Hanlan.

The setup was perfect, but there was a swift anticlimax. Martin got cold feet and never showed up to stick the gun in the lady's ribs.

Hanlan's explanations of these events at the SIC's hearings were hard to follow. He said that Figliuzzi had planned a purse-snatching, not a payroll heist. He said that he, Hanlan, had really planned to arrest Figliuzzi when the crime was committed. But he admitted that he had never reported the robbery plans, about which Figliuzzi had supposedly informed him in advance, to his superiors. Purse-snatching, Hanlan explained, was not really a crime worth worrying about—"I don't think it is serious to snatch a purse and run. Kids are doing it every day in the street."

The more prosperous the syndicates became the more deeply their power networks reached into civic life and municipal government. Increasingly any policeman who wanted to fight gambling found resistance, not only within the force, but from largely inscrutable areas of higher power. In Yonkers, supervision of the police department, the fire department, the city jail, and certain licensing functions is vested in a commissioner of public safety. From

1948 to 1952 the police department of Yonkers mounted an active program to combat syndicated gambling and crime. The program included the use of legalized wiretaps against gambling syndicates on a sustained and coordinated basis, along with the use of informants and a well-developed program of liaison and coordination within the department. The program was under the direction of Captain Edward M. Otis.

In 1952 a new commissioner of public safety, Milton E. Goldman, was appointed. Shortly thereafter Otis was ordered to turn over his wiretap equipment to the deputy commissioner, and was assigned to a desk job completely removed from organized crime and antigambling activities. The program was dismantled, and, during the ensuing ten years, while a vast increase occurred in syndicated gambling and crime in Yonkers, it was never reinstituted.

On January 16, 1958, Frank E. Vescio was appointed a captain in the department and was assigned to the command of Precinct 2. A month later state police, operating over the heads of the Yonkers force, raided a multimillion-dollar policy bank in Yonkers. Commissioner Goldman reacted immediately. A well-publicized meeting of all police captains was held at City Hall and Commissioner Goldman told them that he wanted the law enforced. The captains were told that they would be held responsible for conditions in their precinct. They were ordered to make arrests and to cooperate with any outside agency working on the problem. However, no guidance, direction, leadership, or planning of any kind was offered or suggested. The older captains on the force told Captain Vescio that the meeting was really a kind of window dressing and that they intended to conduct business as usual.

Vescio, however, told the SIC that he took Goldman at

his word and started a campaign to enforce gambling laws in the second precinct. Using previous arrest records as an initial source and assigning a patrolman as his aide in the program, he made a series of raids that resulted in sixteen arrests. Within a few months he had all but closed down gambling in his precinct.

Reaction came swiftly. A city councilman had a talk with Vescio. The councilman said that second-precinct gamblers had been complaining bitterly about the treatment they had been receiving since Vescio took charge. "It is too bad," Vescio replied. "I am doing my job."

Relying on Goldman's orders to "work with outside agencies if necessary," Vescio began a cooperative program with the district attorney that quickly resulted in new major arrests. Vescio did not notify his superiors in the department about the operations with the DA because the DA instructed him not to do so. Vescio shared the DA's distrust of the department's high brass; he had found from prior experience that "there was a leak someplace."

This was apparently too much for Goldman. Vescio stated to the commission that after he and the DA conducted an especially successful raid, Goldman called Vescio in, chewed him out, and threatened departmental action against him for cooperating with the DA. It soon became clear that Vescio was a marked man.

Q. Captain, what happened to you after that meeting which you have described, as far as your life in the department was concerned?

A. In the course of my travels, of course, you pick up information through the grapevine, and I was getting information from friends of mine that after election I would be out of the Second Precinct; that apparently I was stepping on too

many people's toes . . . that right after election I was going
to get the hell out of there.

Q. And it did happen?

A. Yes.

Goldman waited until after elections, then removed
Vescio from command of the second precinct and transferred him to the communications, records and training
division and to the repair shop. These assignments removed him from any active law-enforcement function. It is
normal procedure in the department for each captain to
be assigned a car for performance of his duties. As a last
little touch, Captain Vescio also had his car taken away
from him. Vescio complained angrily and in due time a car
was found for him—a 1953 Ford, the oldest car in the
department.

Meanwhile, state police continued their embarrassing
activity of raiding Yonkers gambling joints over the heads
of the local police. After each such raid the regular pattern
would ensue. The captains were called in by Goldman,
berated, scolded, accused of being incompetent, corrupt,
or inefficient, and told to make gambling arrests. Goldman's
statements always received wide publicity. But the SIC
states that specific recommendations for an antigambling
program made by the captains were ignored by the commissioner and his deputy, neither of whom ever followed
up the commissioner's own highly publicized remarks with
any kind of leadership, guidance, or direction of their own.
There was, said Captain Vescio, a double standard that
everyone understood—"something for the public, and an
unwritten law behind the scenes."

"What was the unwritten law?" the State Investigation
Commission asked Vescio.

"Don't do what you are told to do," Vescio replied. "If you make gambling arrests you are a stiff, you should know better."

Goldman himself followed up the reassignment of Vescio and the public berating of the captains for their gambling ineffectiveness by appointing to his own office Lt. Andrew Sutton. During a 1956 investigation a Westchester County grand jury reported that "some police officers were associating and fraternizing with known bookmakers and gamblers." At that time Commissioner Goldman had identified Sutton as one of the officers in question, and the SIC found that he had continued his contacts with gamblers after going to work for Goldman. In the public hearings, Goldman denied that anyone in the city government had suggested that he appoint Sutton. In the private hearings he sang a slightly different tune, admitting that several persons had suggested Sutton's appointment:

Q. Were they people involved in local politics in any way?
A. Some were, some were not.
Q. Could you tell us who the people were who were involved in politics who recommended Sutton to you?
A. I couldn't say at this time.
Q. Is it that you do not wish to say or that you don't remember?
A. It is not a question that I don't wish to say. I can't quote who spoke to me in his behalf at this time.
Q. Is it anyone holding political office in the City of Yonkers?
A. It may have been. I can't say yes or no to that.

At the public hearings one of the commissioners asked Goldman about the flat contradiction in his public and his private testimony. Goldman proved imperturbable:

Q. Of course, what puzzles us here frankly, Commissioner, is that at the time you were asked the identical question, was he recommended by anyone, you said, by several. Now you were asked was he recommended by anyone, and you said no. Those two answers to me are frankly not consistent, just as many of your answers have not been consistent. Go on.

A. I am not a consistent man.

After its hearings the commission made many recommendations, some of them aimed at the central problem of the disarray of the numerous separate law-enforcement bodies in the county. A key recommendation was to consolidate the thirty-nine different police forces into one county-wide force. Even if the other reforms it had recommended were made, the commission said, "essentially the same basic system of multi-department, fragmented law enforcement would prevail," unless this were done. The suggestion was not well received in most quarters. "A county department would be ridiculous," said Mayor Joseph P. Vaccarella of Mount Vernon. "We are capable of handling our own police problems. I am absolutely against interference from the outside." A veteran traffic policeman in White Plains showed the never-failing realism of small-town forces: "It'll never happen here so long as there are forty chiefs and more than forty commissioners to fight it off, and forty-five county supervisors and a backfield of state senators and assemblymen to help them block it at Albany [the state capital]." Another White Plains policeman reflected the extent to which corruption had become accepted as a way of life: "What earthly good could a county department be? The policy-slip and horse-room boys would then have to reach only one chief, one commissioner."

One city has been taking the problem seriously. The city of New Rochelle interviewed forty-five highly qualified candidates, and on May 1, 1964, hired Edward F. Carey, former commander of North Brooklyn detectives on the New York City force and a well-known nemesis of gambling and narcotics rings, to fill the newly created $20,000 post of New Rochelle police commissioner. Carey faces the hardest assignment of his career. North Brooklyn may have been tough, but green, quiet Westchester County is probably tougher.

CHAPTER SEVEN

Triumph and Tragedy in Indianapolis

Lieutenant John Kestler stepped out from behind his desk and walked over to the wall, where two large maps of the city of Indianapolis were dotted with pins of various colors.

"This one," he said, "shows a series of taxicab holdups. The first one occurred on January 9. A few days later another one occurred in the same vicinity, at about the same time of night. The two cabdrivers gave descriptions of the holdup man that didn't fully coincide, but when the reports came across my desk I thought it might be the same man. A few nights later there was a third holdup. Then I began to keep this map."

A group of yellow pins had been stuck into the map, most of them clustered in an area a little west of the center of town. Several blocks to the north there was another cluster of red pins. There was a scattering of both red and yellow pins in other areas, but they were largely concentrated in these two spots.

"The yellow pins," Lieutenant Kestler explained, "show where the cabs were picked up. The red ones show where the holdups took place. We moved more men and cars into the two areas, and set up what we call a stakeout. In plain language, we lay for him. Unmarked patrol cars cruised through the areas. Patrolmen went out on the streets in all kinds of disguises. Some wore business suits. Others wore paint-stained clothing. Some stood around at bus stops. They all kept their eyes peeled, and they all carried transistor radios. In a couple of weeks we nailed the guy, and when he saw this map he confessed to the whole string of holdups. In the old days no one analyzed reports as they came in with an eye for patterns. The result was, unless someone just happened to notice a pattern, a series of robberies could occur, and each one might be handled and investigated as an individual case."

The other map was marked "Mutt and Jeff." The pins on this map were clustered in the southern end of town.

"This is a current case," said Lieutenant Kestler. "We haven't nailed Mutt and Jeff yet."

On March 1 a dry-cleaning establishment in the southern end of town was held up by two armed men, one tall and one short. Two nights later there was another holdup, this time of a small bakery. One of the two robbers in this holdup was noticeably taller than the other. On the second holdup one of the men was wearing sun glasses and the other was reported as a blond, whereas both men in the dry-cleaning holdup were reported as having black hair. But Lieutenant Kestler thought that they might be the same men, with one of them dyeing his hair and the other using sun glasses to throw the police off. A couple of nights later there was a third holdup. It fitted the pattern—two men, one taller than the other, both of them masked this time, holding up a small establishment in the south end of town between 8:30 and 10:00 in the evening. Lieutenant Kestler started the Mutt and Jeff map, and plans were made for a stakeout.

"The guys are still pulling these holdups with various disguises, but they aren't fooling anybody and they won't last much longer," said Lieutenant Kestler. "Almost always, they pick on small establishments, just around closing hour in the evening, when there might be just one clerk in the store. I wouldn't be surprised if we nailed them tonight, or at least sometime this week."

Lieutenant Kestler went back to his desk and sat down. "That's one of the functions of this new planning division," he said. "We watch for patterns. Where the same man, or same group of men, or the same gang, are pulling a series of crimes, they almost always run some kind of pattern. When we spot the pattern, that makes our response faster and surer. It may be the type of person or store that he attacks. It may be the geographical location, the time of day or night, or any of a number of other things.

"There are also patterns in the descriptions that witnesses give," Lieutenant Kestler added. "A woman is usually far more reliable than a man in reporting color of eyes and color of hair, but she will usually overestimate height. A man in a certain line of business will be able to describe the type of wearing apparel with which he is familiar. A shoe salesman, in many cases, can tell you not only the color, but the brand name of a holdup man's shoes. And any man that holds up a clothing store would be wise to change his entire style of dress from that night on. The descriptions of wearing apparel that clothing salesmen give are quite often detailed and reliable."

"Considering that the planning division is hardly a year old," I said, "you certainly seem to have a good operation."

"Well," he replied, "it is having an impact already. Everyone feels that it's one of the best things to come out of the Indiana study."

Lieutenant Kestler and the members of the Indianapolis police force who work with him are officers of whom any city could be proud. Talking with him, it was hard to re-member that their work was being carried out in the shadow of a scandal that had made national headlines just three weeks before.

If any town exemplifies the spirit and virtues of Middle Western America, it is Indianapolis. Capital of Indiana and the national headquarters of the American Legion, it has a fraternal spirit, a civic pride, and a friendliness that one feels from the day one arrives in town. The people of the city—unlike the people of most cities—have long taken great interest and pride in their police force. Basking in strong civic support, the force was handsome, strong, and, apparently, highly efficient. The motorcycle corps of the Indianapolis force was undoubtedly one of the finest in the nation. More important, the crime rate in the city, as reflected in the statistics reported to the FBI by the police department, was substantially below that of most other American cities of comparable size. There seemed to be every justification for the feeling of satisfaction, and even smugness, that the people felt about their police. Other cities might be having problems of police corruption, but not Indianapolis.

When the great police scandal broke in Chicago in 1960, Indianapolis took the occasion for a moment of calm self-congratulation. "Police department scandals such as those in Chicago aren't likely to occur in Indianapolis, police and city officials predicted confidently today," said a story in the Indianapolis *News*. "Chief deterrents to corruption in the Indianapolis force, officers say, are: (1) Prompt elimination of 'bad apples' from the Police Department. (2) Constant investigation of complaints about police, no matter how minor."

Checks and balances; protection for career officers; strict

supervision by men of integrity—these, said the city fathers, were the foundations on which good police work and freedom from scandal were based. They were unprepared for the possibility that the opening wedge for evil might be found in such sophisticated areas as defects of administration and badly thought-out structures of command.

In 1961 police scandals erupted in other cities, including the Buffalo scandal described in another chapter of this book. Indianapolis still felt no premonition. In 1962 civic pride in the police was reflected in the opening of a magnificent new police headquarters building, constructed as part of a new complex of municipal offices. By this time, however, the first doubts had begun to appear.

In rapid succession, a number of women were beaten and robbed in the streets of the city at night. Police seemed something less than effective in dealing with the rash of crime. Reporters from the Indianapolis *Star* and the Indianapolis *News* dug into police records and published series of headline articles on what seemed to them to be obvious patterns of crime in the city. One of these reporters coined the phrase "the streets of fear," and the term stuck. The police were probably not as ineffective as these articles may have implied, but public confidence had received its first jolt.

The reporters noticed something else. Several of the crimes which they had been investigating had apparently never found their way into the official police tabulations of crime in the city. In one case, a woman, walking on the street near the center of town early in the evening, was struck from behind and her purse was grabbed. She was taken to the hospital, remained there for a week, and died from the effects of the assault. A reporter found that when she died the case had not yet been entered as an assault and robbery in the police department's crime tally.

Looking into the way in which the police department was set up, the reporters noticed that each division in the department seemed to run with great autonomy. There were eleven different division heads, with no common superior other than the chief himself. Among the autonomous divisions was the vice squad. True, no one knew of any scandal, or any hint of scandal, in the squad.

After the newspaper stories two things promptly happened which reflected the deep loyalty of the city toward its police. The Federation of Women's Clubs decided to pool its resources for an anti-crime crusade to be carried out in cooperation with the police department. The group launched several programs. It conducted a study of street lighting, then worked with the police and the city administration to get the necessary appropriations to improve lighting in inadequately lighted areas. A large-scale program for working with high school drop-outs was begun, to help them to find constructive work and to encourage them to return to school. A committee of court watchers was created, and at least one member of the committee was present in the courtroom during numerous trials and proceedings. The observations and reports of these committee members were passed on to the membership of all the clubs in the federation.

The group also felt strong concern for the problem of the relatively low social prestige of police work. Among other things, they instituted a program of teas and social receptions honoring the wives of the city's policemen.

Meanwhile, discussions were also going on in the Indianapolis Chamber of Commerce. Law enforcement had always been a high-priority civic interest of the chamber.

After conferring with police officials, the chamber announced on July 1, 1962, that it would set up a new unit to study and throw a continuous public spotlight on all phases of law enforcement in the city. The announcement was welcomed by police officials. Mr. Layton E. Kincannon, vice president of Rock Island Refining Company, and one of the city's most respected civic leaders, agreed to serve as chairman. Mr. Donald W. Ruby, a crime reporter for the Indianapolis *Star,* was chosen as full-time salaried staff director of the law-enforcement committee.

One of the first things the committee did was to arrange for Mr. Kincannon, Mr. Ruby, Mayor Albert H. Losche, and the safety board president, David M. Silver, to visit St. Louis to look over its recently reorganized police department. The group was deeply impressed with what it saw in St. Louis. The whole structure of the St. Louis department had been changed and modernized, and it was difficult to avoid the realization that the internal structure of the Indianapolis department resembled the old St. Louis setup under which a major scandal had occurred. The mayor, Mr. Silver, Mr. Ruby, and Mr. Kincannon all wondered whether it might not be a good idea to have the Indianapolis department surveyed before disaster struck, instead of waiting for a scandal and calling in the experts after it happened.

The idea was reinforced by more discoveries that were being made within the department about its statistical reporting. Noel A. Jones, a thirty-three-year veteran of the force, had just taken over as captain of the detective bureau. He found, as the reporters had found, that many crimes were not being properly tabulated for the statistical report submitted annually to the FBI. The apparently low crime rate of which the city had been so proud began to look like a statistical mirage.

The chamber of commerce officially recommended that a survey of the department be made. The recommendation had the approval of the department and of the newspapers and civic groups. The city administration made inquiry of the Police Services Group of Indiana University. The PSG agreed to do the job, and public interest ran high as the survey team arrived in March 1963.

The five-man team was headed by Robert P. Shumate, director of the university's Police Services Group and former assistant director for research and development for the International Association of Chiefs of Police. Lawrence E. Brown, assistant professor in the university's Department of Police Administration, is a former FBI agent and a lawyer. James W. Osterberg, an associate professor in the department, is a former New York City policeman, a former faculty member of the Baruch School of Public Administration of the City University of New York, and coauthor of the standard work, *An Introduction to Criminalistics*. Richard A. Myren, another associate professor, formerly police consultant to the U.S. Children's Bureau, is a specialist in problems of juvenile crime. James R. Dirksen, an electronic data-processing expert, had been data-processing supervisor in the Human Resources Research Office at George Washington University and a consultant on data processing for the International Association of Chiefs of Police before joining the Indiana faculty.

Survey teams of this kind are something new in police work in the United States. They reflect a gulf between the growth of modern scientific criminology and what most of the nation's police forces are actually doing. It took a nationwide series of police scandals, many of which are described in this book, to dramatize this widening gulf.

Things have been made worse by the fact that the science of police work has been as much an orphan in the academic world as it has been in city budgets. Most academicians have regarded police work as beneath the dignity of their degrees and their training. A lot of the recent pioneering in modern scientific police work has therefore been done by present or former members of police forces who worked their way up the academic ladder the hard way —getting bachelor's degrees, law degrees, and even master's and doctorate degrees on their own while pounding beats or riding in squad cars at night. In the past five years they have suddenly found themselves in the vanguard of a big new academic field. Programs in scientific criminology have been launched or greatly expanded by professional groups such as the International Association of Chiefs of Police. A number of universities, such as Michigan, Northwestern, Indiana, and California, now have full-scale degree programs in police work and criminology.

The best of the new group of experts find themselves in great demand. There simply aren't enough of them to go around. After being snapped up by professional groups or universities they often find themselves tapped to conduct surveys designed to close the generation-wide gap between police practice and progress in criminology.

In the 1950's Indiana University began offering night courses for policemen in major Indiana cities where it has extension centers. In 1958 it opened such a program in Indianapolis, offering a series of consecutive courses in police administration, traffic investigation, criminal investigation, case preparation, and court procedure. Policemen attending the classes had to do it on their own time and pay the cost of tuition and books themselves. The university expected seven or eight cops to enroll. On opening night forty showed up, completely swamping the facilities, and enthusiasm and enrollment have continued and increased. No one had dreamed that such a desire for professional education existed among members of the force.

Back at the main campus in Bloomington the Department of Police Administration continued to generate ideas. In 1962 the university set up its Police Services Group to provide experts and survey teams to police departments throughout the nation. "The staff of PSG," said the university's announcement, "is comprised of a central core of former police officers from the municipal, state and federal level now with the faculty of the University, and experts from such diversified fields as mathematics, data processing, economics, and government. Complementing this permanent staff are a number of resource consultants who are drawn either from the faculties of related departments within the University or from a group of non-university experts who are on an established retainer basis with PSG. These consultants are recognized authorities in public administration, budget control, traffic, and personnel selection." What it amounted to was that the university was marshaling the full weight of its facilities, resources, and prestige behind its police program—a revolutionary reversal of prevailing academic attitudes of the very recent past.

When the survey team began its work in Indianapolis, it quickly became interested in the problem that had been touched on by a newspaper reporter who had noticed that the vice squad seemed to be running a little empire of its own. Like most police forces, the Indianapolis force had grown like Topsy, and had divisions sprouting all over the place with little coordination and no real supervision. The structure, in other words, was a mess. Dull stuff to old-time pistol packers, maybe. But, as the survey team knew only too well, and the people of Indianapolis were soon to find out, it is the dull stuff out of which sensational things are born.

As we have noted, the force's eleven sections and divisions were pretty much minding their own business, and each had no common superior other than the chief, to whom the head of each section or division reported directly. The men on the beat and in the cars were divided into three eight-hour shifts. Each shift had its own commander, did things its own way, and had no common supervisor or coordinator except the chief. Each of the three shifts kept records and passed information on to the others, but they had no coordinated programs or plans for dealing with crime. The traffic division was a division entirely separate from the three shifts, doing its own work under its own commander, and responsible only to the chief. On the investigative side there were a vice division and a homicide division, each having equal status with the detective division. Each of the three divisions had its own commander, did things its own way, and was responsible only to—the chief.

The Indianapolis Police Department was thus being run under a sort of articles of confederation. The effects had bitten deep. Men on the three shifts did little or nothing about vice violations that they spotted. It wasn't their province and they knew that the vice division wouldn't thank them for butting in. The same held for traffic violations and vehicle accidents. The traffic division had its own squad cars, painted white, and even its own uniforms. It was proud—and rather jealous—of its prerogatives and its domain. "Regular cops" paid little attention to traffic matters. When a cop on one of the three shifts came upon a traffic accident, he would radio in for a "traffic car." The traffic car might take twenty minutes to arrive, but accident investigation was their job and they wanted to do it. Cops on the three shifts also paid little attention to traffic violations; that was another job for the "traffic guys," not the "felony cops." "It had gotten to the point," said one patrolman, "where people felt that cops in the black patrol cars wouldn't bother them. The only ones they had to watch out for were the white traffic cars."

The survey team saw the truth and told it—police work in Indianapolis was out of control. It recommended complete reorganization of the department, putting all the uniformed force under a deputy chief for operations and all the investigative force under a deputy chief for investigation. The number of men reporting directly to the chief would be cut from eleven to four—the two deputy chiefs, the head of training and inspection, and the head of a proposed executive division which would include a planning branch and a statistics tabulating branch. Existing operations divisions, such as the three shifts and traffic, would be reduced to branches under the operations deputy. Homicide and vice would become branches within the investigative division, which would include the detectives.

Other criticisms were made and changes proposed as the survey progressed. Detective work, it said, was poor, and records kept by the division were inadequate—a fact that the newly appointed detective bureau captain, Noel Jones, had already discovered. The team also cast a cool eye on the vaunted motorcycle corps. Motorcycle cops, it pointed out, are most efficient in good weather, least efficient in bad weather when the need for police was often greater. It recommended cutting the corps to half its 1963 size.

The list of recommendations piled up—by the end of the survey there were 119 of them. Many were the old ways that the survey team thought should be consigned to the scrap heap. Many were the new, unfamiliar tricks that would have to be learned by people who were quite comfortable the way things were. Many were the feudal toes that would be trod upon. Long and loud were the cries of anguish.

"Styles of police work are hard to change," Lieutenant Kestler said when we talked about it nearly a year later. "I worked with the survey group in studying some areas of the department. We would come upon a set of records which were being neatly and conscientiously kept. The survey team would ask what they were being used for. Nobody knew. Then we would check all around the department to see if any use of them was being made anywhere. No use was being made of them. Still, they were being kept because they had always been kept as far back as anybody could remember and it never occurred to anybody to assess their value and suggest that they be eliminated.

"That's one of the useful functions of outside surveys," he added thoughtfully. "The outside people come in, and they have no commitment to the way things are, and no axe to grind other than getting things to run the best way possible. Community interest in the survey runs high, and the recommendations carry a weight of public opinion with them that you wouldn't get on proposals coming from the inside. Changes of the kind that were recommended for this force wouldn't have had a prayer of getting anywhere if they had been recommended by someone inside."

The twin weights of inertia and the resistance of petty empires to change are often strong enough to offset even these advantages of an outside survey. In Denver many of the principal recommendations produced by a costly survey made by a top-notch team from the IACP have been buried or junked. In New Rochelle, New York, the recommendations of a police expert, brought in to recommend reforms in the department, were given decent burial. "Everyone was anxious to forget about it," New Rochelle's city manager said in 1963. "It was shelved, period."

In Indianapolis the pressures resisting change were powerful and would easily have prevailed over a less determined city administration and police chief. Empires like the traffic division had plenty of friends in the highest places. Three former mayors of Indanapolis banded together and issued a public statement opposing the survey team's recommendation that the traffic division be downgraded to a branch, placing it under the new deputy chief for operations, and integrating its work into that of the rest of the uniformed force. Homicide Captain Randolph Schubert strongly protested turning his autonomous division into a branch that would coordinate with other investigative branches. The mayors and Captain Schubert all stated that they believed that better and more efficient police work could be done under the existing structure than under the proposed changes. But the mayor and council of Indianapolis were fully committed to backing the survey recommendations. All the major changes in structure recommended by the Indiana team were made.

The team was careful to avoid one common pitfall of such surveys. Often a survey team will, after spending many months on a job, write up a massive report containing all its recommendations, dump it in one indigestible lump into the laps of the city administration, and depart. Taken all at once, the team's findings and recommendations contain more practical and conceptual changes than can be easily grasped. Meanwhile, public interest has usually waned. In the end the report is often quietly filed, and the forces of inertia and vested interest win easily. Working closely with top police officers and with the city government, the Indiana survey team did its work in six stages and submitted a series of six reports, each covering an understandable, limited segment of the total problem. The major recommendations that met the approval of the city officials were implemented as each report was issued and while the survey team was still present to advise and help. At the end of the survey the team conducted two weeks of eight-hour-a-day classes for nearly everyone on the force with the rank of sergeant or above, to familiarize them with the ideas and procedures of the new way.

"It's interesting," said Lieutenant Kestler. "When a new thing is proposed to one division, it is resisted. But then when the division tries it, likes it, and finds that it works, the rest want to try the new way too. Soon everybody begins to feel a big change of mood, and there is a feeling of interest and excitement."

Lieutenant Kestler's planning division, whose creation was among the initial suggestions of the survey team, was set up experimentally in April 1963 and put on an official, permanent basis in November. Reports on all phases of the force's work go through the division. It watches for patterns, coordinates programs, marshals forces to meet new problems, studies trends—and thinks. "For example," said Lieutenant Kestler, "we started to study reports of auto accidents. That used to be the sole province of the traffic division. When there was a rise in the accident rate, traffic would tell its men to get out there and make more speeding arrests. We have been analyzing accident reports as they come in and we find that speeding is way down the list as a cause of traffic accidents in Indianapolis. Improper turns are by far the biggest single cause. Next comes tailgating—riding too close to the car ahead. This is the kind of information we want to get out both to the men on the force and to the public."

The planning division is making some other discoveries. They have been analyzing reports of work done by patrol cars, and have broken down the work into nine categories, from the most serious to the least serious types of crime. Category 8 is for extremely minor matters barely within a reasonable definition of police work, and category 9 is for work that is not genuine police work at all. "Things like helping elderly people in and out of bed, dog-bite reports, cats up trees, abandoned bicycles, people with cash who ask to be escorted to the bank—these things go into categories 8 and 9," Lieutenant Kestler explained. So far, 83 percent of all the work done by the patrol cars falls into these two categories! "It deserves a lot of thought," said Lieutenant Kestler. "There is a big clamor in this city, and in other cities, that there aren't enough police. Maybe there *are* enough police, and they're not being used properly."

An apparently odd result of Indianapolis' year of courage and triumph in police reform was that the crime rate went up. In part, this reflected the nationwide rise in the crime rate which has been continuing for many years. But it also reflected the fact that crime statistics were being more accurately and thoroughly reported. Detective Captain Noel Jones began to reform the statistical procedures in 1962 and the system was improved and refined during and after the survey. The 1963 figures show a 16 percent increase in reported crime over 1962. The actual rise was probably well below the 10 percent national average. In making its city-by-city comparison of 1962 and 1963 crime rates in major cities, the FBI says of Indianapolis, "1962 figures not comparable to 1963," and omits the 1962 statistics.

The change in the setup of the traffic department, which

encountered especially stout resistance, has produced spectacular results. Arrests for traffic violations for January-February 1964 increased 44 percent over the same period in 1963, while accidents decreased by 6½ percent.

Some problems remain beyond the power of the survey team or the force to solve—the most serious being the unwillingness of the public to pay properly for police work. A uniformed patrolman in Indianapolis starts at $5,000 a year. After the first year he gets a $200 raise. Another $300 is tacked on after he has completed his fifth year, and after each succeeding five years he gets another raise of $100. Thus, a patrolman who has served on the force for ten years gets $5,600. A lieutenant on the force starts at $6,000. The chief got $9,600 before the survey; he now gets $12,000. The impact of this is felt in recruiting. "Why would a bright, intelligent man want to go into police work in this city?" a patrolman asked me. "A good, able person can look forward to earning between $40,000 to $70,000 as a top executive with, for example, various utility companies in this city with as few as 200 employees. There are 904 men on the Indianapolis force, and I'm darned sure that the demands of the work at the top level are greater than the demands made on most executives of those utilities."

In the November 1963 elections Indianapolis got a new mayor, John J. Barton, a former career policeman with the Indiana State Police who had just completed a term as superintendent of the state police force. When he took office in January he appointed a new chief of the Indianapolis force—Noel A. Jones, the hard-driving, dedicated head of the detective division, who was as close to being everybody's police hero as a man could come. The city and the force could afford to be proud of what it had achieved in the past year, and with Barton and Jones running things there was no doubt that reform would continue to be carried out with energy and intelligence. But already there were signs that the effort had come too late.

On June 8, 1963, while the survey was in progress, two cars pulled up in front of the expensive home of Isaac "Tuffy" Mitchell at 21 West Kesset Boulevard. Three men stepped out of one of the cars and mounted the slope of the lawn to where the fifty-year-old Mitchell was standing, clad only in a pair of blue plaid shorts, watering his lawn. Mitchell turned the hose to one side to look at the badges that the men presented. They were T-men—special agents of the United States Treasury Department.

At the same moment, a total of 130 T-men stepped into ten other homes and business locations in Indianapolis and showed their badges. The raids had been coordinated to the second by the use of walkie-talkie radio, to prevent word of arrests from spreading in time for evidence to be destroyed. The planning and setting up of the raids had been kept a complete secret, and not even the Indianapolis police knew about it until it happened. The raids were such a surprise to Indianapolis police that they towed away the automobile of one of the agents participating in the raids—it was parked in a no-parking area.

After the agents arrested Mitchell the group went into the house. The agents showed Mitchell search warrants and asked him to open his safe. Inside they found $3,800 in cash and a detailed set of records on a large illegal gambling empire. The agents then searched the house and property with painstaking care. They found additional records behind a secret panel in the basement, in an upstairs bedroom, and in secret panels in Mitchell's car. They showed him to be the kingpin of a million-dollar-a-year gambling ring in Indianapolis that hired 450 numbers writers, had 11 runners, and kept a full-time staff that handled daily records.

Late that night the T-men marched their prisoners into federal court. As the group passed, a janitor shook his head sadly. "I haven't got a chance of winning today," he murmured within hearing of a reporter.

The janitor knew where he could go to participate in illegal gambling. The question was, why didn't the police know? Reporters besieged Mayor Albert H. Losche at his home, by phone. Losche admitted that he was "surprised" by the raids and that he had known nothing about them until they had taken place. A reporter pointed out that Mitchell, alleged kingpin of the operation, was a holder of a federal gambling stamp, and that this fact had been prominently publicized in the Indianapolis *Star*. "I presume things like that do get by, and I guess they [the Treasury agents] learn about them through their gambling stamps," the confused Losche said. Asked if the police did not know that Mitchell held a federal stamp, Losche said that he guessed they must have known.

For the police it was a hard and embarrassing blow. But a still grimmer turn of events lay ahead. For sheer dynamite, nothing that the Treasury agents found in Tuffy Mitchell's house and car compared to the ten-inch strip of adding-machine tape that they found in his wallet. Beside the figures on this tape, a number of names had been written in red ink.

In January 1964 a Marion County grand jury was convened, and it looked at that tape. It subsequently subpoenaed twenty-seven members of the Indianapolis force, including a number of officers and men of the formerly free-wheeling vice division.

On the afternoon of March 31, 1964, Chief Jones excused all twenty-seven men from service and told them to wait in a room on the second floor of the police building.

About 2:30 P.M. Deputy County Prosecutor John Davis appeared before Judge Eugene M. Fife at criminal court and handed him the results of the grand jury's investigation. It was a sheaf of twenty-three indictments. Fife looked them over. "Twenty-two of these men appear to be Indianapolis policemen," Judge Fife said. "Yes, your honor," Davis replied, "they are."

The names on the adding-machine tape, said the indictments, were the names of Indianapolis policemen, and the figures showed how much they were being paid to protect illegal gambling in Indianapolis. Those indicted included captains, lieutenants, and sergeants. Only three of the indicted men were patrolmen.

Fife retired to his chambers with Judge Saul I. Rabb and several court clerks to prepare the arrest orders, while County Prosecutor Noble R. Pearcy called Chief Jones and told him the news.

Chief Jones put down the phone, and walked slowly up the stairs to the second floor. There he told the men which of them had been indicted. "On what charge?" one of them asked. Jones had forgotten to ask. He called Pearcy back. "The charge is bribery," he said as he put down the phone. He ordered the twenty-two indicted men to go to the county jail to be fingerprinted and to await arrest.

Chief Jones returned to his office and soon was being interviewed by reporters. "This is more than bribery of policemen," he said. "It's an indictment of our community."

While he was answering questions, tears came to his eyes. "I'm sorry to be this way," he apologized, "but I never knew a more discouraging day."

CHAPTER EIGHT

Boston, Illinois State Police, New York City

Until 1963 the mayor of Boston did not even appoint the city's police commissioner—he was appointed by the governor of Massachusetts. This was just one anomaly in a city and a state that are both political museums. They are also probably the most corrupt city and state in the nation. Hardly a month goes by when a new scandal does not erupt in the city of Boston or in the Massachusetts state government. "Politics in Massachusetts are essentially feudal and tribalistic. . . . Like his predecessors, Democratic Governor Endicott Peabody reigns but does not rule over a chaotic collection of Executive Councillors, autonomous commissioners, and semi-independent department heads, many of whom he did not appoint and cannot dismiss. This archaic diffusion of power, compounded by human greed, is one of the root causes of the corruption which has made the image of Massachusetts so unsavory in the nation." *

With monotonous regularity, engineers and construction firms in Massachusetts bribe legislators and highway officials to obtain contracts. Judges award trusteeships to relatives and friends. Real-estate men deal with themselves as official assessors. In cases described by Sheehan in his

* Edward R. F. Sheehan, "Brooke of Massachusetts," *Harper's* (June, 1964), p. 41.

Harper's article, a state representative, convicted of larceny, was reelected while still in jail. A city official was dismissed following the disclosure that he had been purchasing municipal property at bargain rates that he himself established. A consulting engineer, an attorney, a state official, and a judge were all convicted in 1963 of embezzling nearly $800,000 of public funds in connection with the construction of the Boston Common Underground Garage. A state adviser was recently convicted of soliciting bribes. At this writing, more than a score of indictments against important public officials for conspiracy, bribery, and larceny are pending. More will probably be generated by investigations currently under way.

In such a situation police corruption becomes a function of general civic rottenness. Boston has not suffered from a shortage of professional advice in the running of its police department. It has probably had more such help in past years than any other major city, according to a 1962 statement by Quinn Tamm, executive director of the International Association of Chiefs of Police, but it has made little use of the advice. One such survey was done by Bruce Smith of the Institute of Public Administration in 1949. Recommendations included such things as consolidation of police stations and the establishment of a personnel bureau headed by a trained civilian. These and other recommendations were not implemented; like many cities, Boston paid for the survey and quietly filed away the report.

After being appointed by the governor, with the advice and consent of the governor's executive council, for a seven-year term, the commissioner was not accountable to the governor for his day-to-day activity. The accountability decreased even further when the governor who had appointed the commissioner left office. The mayor of Boston had even less control over the police commissioner. The commissioner, for his part, had the right to "requisition" the money he needed from the city treasury. Only on pay increases or increases in the size of the force was he required to consult the governor. The commissioner's accountability to the taxpayers of Boston was nil. This setup was designed some time in the dim past to "keep the department out of politics," but of course it did not do this. Police Commissioner Leo J. Sullivan was the Boston campaign manager for Governor Foster Furcolo. When Furcolo was elected, he appointed Sullivan as Boston police commissioner, and Sullivan retained the office when Furcolo left the governor's chair.

On November 30, 1961 CBS-TV aired a nationwide television show entitled "Biography of a Bookie Joint." Acting on a tip, CBS news cameramen had set up concealed cameras in a building opposite a shop in the Back Bay area of Boston. During a surveillance of several weeks the cameramen took pictures of ten different Boston policemen entering the shop, apparently to make bets or receive rake-offs. The program caused a sensation even in Boston, where it was officially blacked out to protect men who had not yet been tried. Soon after it appeared, Massachusetts Governor John Volpe requested the resignation of Commissioner Sullivan, who had been appointed by his predecessor. Sullivan refused to resign. Formal charges were prepared against him. One of them, arising from the CBS show, charged Sullivan with failing to investigate the alleged misconduct of police officers. By the time the hearing began on February 19, 1962, the Massachusetts Supreme Court had added fuel to the flames by ruling that Sullivan had acted illegally in his assigning of work to private contractors. He had let out the work, the court said, in small, $2,000 contract packages instead of lumping all the work together. Various private sources were awarded these contracts without public bidding. About ninety separate contracts had been let by Commissioner Sullivan in this manner.

In the midst of the ouster hearings, Sullivan resigned. Governor Volpe named Michael J. Cullinane, a career policeman, as the new commissioner, and a bill was introduced in the state legislature to give the mayor of Boston appointment and supervisory power over the city's police commissioner. This legislation finally passed in 1963.

Meanwhile, an International Association of Chiefs of Police survey team was brought in soon after the bookie joint scandal erupted. The survey team made some interesting findings. Instead of being understaffed, the Boston force had 640 more cops than it needed. It was both overstaffed and underpaid. The city had 4.25 policemen per 1,000 population, compared to 2.6 in cities of comparable size. Boston's yearly per capita expenditure for police protection was the highest in the country—$26.19 compared, for example, to New York's $20.69. This great army of men in blue did not combine size with efficiency. Crime in Boston rose 47 percent in the decade of the 1950's while population dropped 13 percent. The IACP found Boston cops doing all kinds of things, such as driving ambulances, taking a yearly census, serving as school-crossing guards, running a taxi licensing bureau, and operating seventeen different police stations, most of which the IACP stated unequivocally could be closed. The survey team recommended reduction of the size of the force by 600 men, saving $3.3 million per year, of which $2 million would be offset by salary increases.

Other things were afoot at the state level. On March 25, 1964, a high official of the Massachusetts State Police was indicted on charges of conspiracy, larceny, aiding and abetting in making false reports, and conflict of interest. Twelve indictments, involving a total of thirty-eight counts, were returned against him. Acting on evidence gathered by the Massachusetts Crime Commission, the Essex County grand jury also indicted four others, including the police official's administrative assistant and two engineering companies. Massachusetts Attorney General Edward A. Brooke told newsmen that the charges involved contracts with several state agencies, including the public works department, the Massachusetts Port Authority, and the Massachusetts Turnpike Authority.

The next day the indicted state police official took a voluntary leave of absence pending the outcome of the indictments. The grand jury's action against him, he said, "had been politically motivated."

On May 11, 1964, the police official was indicted again. He was one of twenty-six persons, including state legislators, and ten corporations who were indicted on various charges of bribery and conspiracy. At this writing the indictments of March 25 and May 11 are still pending. It should be noted that any or all persons or corporations named in these indictments may be found innocent or have the charges against them dismissed at any point during the future course of the cases through the courts.

State police scandals are not common. In certain respects the conditions of state police work are such as to inhibit corruption. State police, covering large areas, do not have the daily, intimate contact with a small group of merchants, gamblers, and criminals that is the lot of the policeman who walks a beat or rides a squad car in a city or town. They therefore do not develop the close and friendly relationships with a small group of people in a small patrol area that opens the door to temptation on both sides. Also, they are largely concerned with what might be called choice police work—patrolling superhighways, investigating accidents, working on major, intercity networks of crime. They have distinctly less of the unpleasant, trivial, or dull kinds of police work that take up much of the city policeman's time. In addition, most state police forces are very well equipped and smartly uniformed. They are usually treated with respect by the average citizen who is inclined to treat his hometown police with anything ranging from condescension to contempt. All these things make for higher prestige, which is reflected in the ability of the state police to maintain high recruiting standards. Many require applicants to have at least two years of college, a requirement that no city police force in the nation could maintain. All these things make for high morale and a high level of professional conduct and performance among state police.

This is not to say that certain paths of temptation are not open to state police, and that these paths have never been trod. A breakdown in effective supervision in certain areas of their geographically large domains is one weakness to which state police are susceptible. When this weakness is combined with certain temptations connected with their highway duties, the worst can happen.

In 1962 whispers began to reach Illinois State Police Chief William Morris about bribery and payoffs in two state police districts, covering a large area south of Chicago. Morris set up a secret inquiry and his investigators promptly came up with something staggering. On the seat of a police car they picked up a little red book in which the methodical state trooper had kept track of payoffs from no fewer than *ninety* trucking firms doing business in and out of Chicago!

The genesis of the payments and the little red book was not hard to figure out, and subsequent detective work confirmed the investigators' suspicions. Like all states, Illinois has maximum weight restrictions on trucks. The purpose of these restrictions is to prevent overloaded trucks from causing undue wear and tear on the state's roads. Studies have shown that road surfaces deteriorate much more swiftly when excessively heavy trucks travel on them. (The truckers themselves call such trucks "highway busters.") This greatly increases the frequency and amount of repair and is therefore costly to taxpayers. It is, however, profitable to trucking companies to overload trucks, since an equivalent amount of material can be moved with fewer trips.

Sometime around 1945 a large number of trucking and construction firms in Chicago decided to solve the problem by "reaching" the state police, who have primary responsibilities for weighing intercity trucks and ticketing violators. In recognition of the burden to the taxpayers that overloaded trucks represent, the state has set heavy penalties for serious infractions. If the overload does not exceed 10,000 pounds, the matter can be brought to a justice of the peace where a modest fine is assessed against the company. If, however, the overload exceeds 10,000 pounds, the case must go to county court where the trucker is liable to a $1,000 fine.

The truckers wanted the state police to overlook most of the instances in which their trucks were found overweight. At such times as the state police did feel obliged to turn a case in, the truckers wanted to be sure that the trooper's arrest ticket showed the amount of overweight to be less than 10,000 pounds. In addition, truckers hoped that the cops would be lenient on myriad other details such as improper license plates and defective equipment.

Approaches were made to the state police, and soon things were arranged. The trucking firms made payments, once or several times a year, on a scale that was graded by rank. In a typical scale, captains got $75, lieutenants got $50, sergeants $25, corporals $15, troopers $10. The pay-offs, in cash or in checks made out to cash with the trucking firm's business card attached by a paper clip, were mailed to the policemen's homes in plain envelopes. With at least ninety companies in on the conspiracy, it takes only a little grade-school arithmetic to figure out the amount by which this supplemented the annual income of the various grades of policemen involved. The trucking companies felt that they were getting what they paid for; the payments were made, faithfully, year after year.

Soon after the little red book was found, Illinois State Director of Public Safety Joseph Regan announced that more than forty of the sixty state police assigned to one of the districts had signed confessions admitting that they had taken payoffs. State officials believe that the payoffs exceeded half a million dollars. These men were promptly suspended, along with their commander.

Twenty state cops were suspended as the investigation continued. Then, a new scandal broke. In November 1963 twenty-three state policemen were suspended on charges of accepting kickbacks from tow-truck operators. The number of accused state troopers soon rose to thirty. Representatives of four towing firms took the Fifth Amendment when summoned to testify before the Illinois Police Merit Board. Others, however, cooperated with the investigators, stating that they usually charged $15 to haul damaged or immobilized cars off state highways, and that 35 percent to 50 percent of this sum was kicked back to state troopers.

"This is a big deal and seems to be more widespread than we anticipated," said Public Safety Director Regan. "There are indications that it has been a common practice in the northeastern Illinois area for a long time." One operator, said Regan, admitted that he had been making the payments for sixteen years, while others had been contributing for "more than ten years." "The kickbacks," said Regan, "apparently ranged from $100 to several thousand dollars a year for each man."

Combing the files of the trucking companies, Regan's investigating team promptly stumbled onto a third scandal. State troopers, it was found, had been signing state credit cards for gas, oil, parts, repairs, and accessories for their private autos. In some fashion, some of these fraudulent sales tickets had found their way into the files of tow-truck companies that had been "doing business" with the cops, and there the investigators found them.

Several features of the Illinois State Police scandals are worth noting. First, when I talked to Public Safety Director Regan, he pointed out that, until fifteen years ago, the Illinois State Police Force was used for political patronage. Jobs and promotions on the force tended to filter through the Illinois state house and legislature. To some extent the recent scandals may be a time bomb planted under the system during the days when some men got on the force and got promotions on the basis of whom they knew, not how qualified they were.

It is clear, too, that the problem of leadership is especially important in state police setups, since geographical isolation makes it possible for many shenanigans to be pulled under an area commander who is either inept or corrupt. All the trouble in Illinois came in certain well-defined geographical areas, covered by specific divisions and units, while other areas and units remained entirely unaffected.

And finally, there is the interesting question of salary. It is generally assumed that state police are better paid than city police, but this is not true. As we shall note later on in this book, the low pay of police does not have so great an impact in producing scandal as is commonly thought, except that it hampers the recruiting of top men and thus plays an important indirect role. But the question of pay cannot be altogether ignored, and it is worth noting that an Illinois state trooper starts at $5,040 a year and goes to a top bracket of $6,060. He shares with almost every other policeman in the nation the status of being a member of a most seriously underpaid profession.

While Illinois and Massachusetts and Boston struggled to untangle their police scandals, the pot began to simmer ominously in New York City. On June 25, 1964, ten New York policemen were dismissed from the force for refusing to sign waivers of immunity in a grand jury investigation of reported payoffs to police by gamblers. Both the State Constitution and the City Charter require dismissal under such circumstances.

New York, the city of big things, has the nation's—and the world's—largest police force. With a strength of 26,000 it is more than double that of Chicago and is five times that of Los Angeles. A patrolman's pay ranges from $6,355 to $7,806 a year.

In 1951 New York produced the biggest police-gambling scandal of modern times. When big-time bookmaker Harry Gross's gambling empire was toppled by federal authorities it was found that he was paying $1 million a year to the police for protection. More than one hundred policemen, implicated in the payoffs, were fired or retired from the force.

Few people, however, believed that the police-gambling alliance had been destroyed.

In 1960 the New York *Post* assigned a team of reporters, led by Ted Poston, to find out what they could about gambling payoffs to the police. The team spent weeks making contacts. They came back with "The Story of The Pad." "It is the story of day-by-day, week-by-week, month-by-month graft which is so vast as to stagger the imagination of the men actually on the take," Ted Poston said in the series.

The *Post*'s police informants and gambling informants agreed on one thing—the magnitude of the operation. "If you knew the actual amount of money involved, you wouldn't believe it," said a police official. "And even if you believed it, the *Post* wouldn't dare print it. The thing is just that big." Other police officials told Poston that some policemen have accumulated so much money from The Pad that they don't know how to spend it without getting in trouble. A former policy banker, shying away from answering specific questions, said, "Look, this thing is much bigger than you think. Anybody who talks about it now is out of business for good. And I'm too old to learn anything else now."

What is The Pad? "It is," said Poston, "the police-approved list of spots or locations where 'official protection' is guaranteed in the six-day-a-week operation of the numbers racket. . . . It can be any agreed-upon place where a numbers player can openly place his daily wager without being molested by the cops . . . each spot must be approved by the police for The Pad. And each spot on The Pad must be paid for in cash."

How are the payoffs made? Poston gave the following as a representative pattern.

(1) The cop on the beat collects an agreed-upon sum, usually $2 a day ($500 a year) from the operator, of each "spot" on his beat that is on The Pad. There are three daily shifts; each cop on each shift collects each day.

(2) The two men in the squad car collect an agreed-upon sum once a week from each "spot" in the area patrolled by their car.

(3) Once a month a "bagman" comes around to each spot to pick up a specified payment to be divided among the higher-ups in the precincts, divisions, and police headquarters who are in on the take.

To operate on a "Full Pad"—that is, to buy complete protection from all three sources—costs each spot about $2,500 a month. Payments are greater for spots that have a larger volume of daily play. Big policy banks handle "action" from 20 or more spots, all on The Pad.

The greed of the cops operating The Pad appeared to be limitless and remorseless. One effect of their tremendous demands was to drive small operators out of business, forcing them to sell out to the bigger operators and to go to work for them. This cleared the field for big-time criminals and national crime syndicates to take over the numbers rackets, which suited the cops fine. The crime syndicates could afford the cops' prices.

One operator who had been forced out of business by excessive police payoff demands said, "There's nothing too complicated about it for the cops. Nobody cheats them. You've got to get on The Pad to stay in business. And if the bite gets too big and drives you out of business, that's just too bad for you." Another stated, "If you write $1,000 worth of numbers a day, then for the first twelve days of the month you work for the cops. The cops are the only ones who are guaranteed to make their taste [profit] no matter what happens."

One policy operator was asked why he bothered to pay off the cop on the beat. "He knows you are on The Pad," the reporter said, "and he knows his superiors may raise hell if he arrests you. So why pay?"

The policy operator smiled at the reporter's naïveté. "Of course he knows he can't arrest me, and I know it too. But he doesn't have to. All he needs to do is just stand in front of my spot and nobody is going to come in and play any numbers as long as a uniformed cop is standing out front."

As Poston and his team of reporters pursued their investigation it became evident that word of their activity had reached unfriendly ears on the force. A former numbers banker now in a legitimate business received a visit from a member of the vice inspector's staff, soon after a *Post* reporter had appeared in his establishment. "If any of you fellows go around shooting off your mouth," said the police officer, "we are going to close down the whole operation." *

Soon after the articles appeared, the New York district attorney's office and the police department began a quiet investigation of payoffs to policemen by racketeers. The investigation proceeded for almost four years, and some breaks finally came. In the spring of 1964 evidence was turned over to two grand juries. On June 25 the story broke when the police department dismissed ten men who

* Poston's article series, a crime-reporting classic, is reprinted in full in *Organized Crime in America*, by Gus Tyler (Ann Arbor, University of Michigan Press, 1962), pp. 260-274.

had refused to sign waivers of immunity to answer questions before one of the juries. One of the ten was a lieutenant attached to the office of Chief Inspector Lawrence J. McKearney, which office was responsible for enforcement of the gambling laws. After the lieutenant had been dismissed Chief McKearney announced the transfer of his entire squad of forty-eight men to other duties throughout the city; the squad, he said, had "lost its effectiveness."

Three days later, in a front-page article in *The New York Times,* reporter Junius Griffin described a payoff by a numbers operator to the police that he had seen on June 1 while doing some background investigating of gambling rackets in Harlem. A numbers banker, dressed in a dark silk suit, entered a Lenox Avenue bar shortly after 1 P.M., went to a quiet corner in the rear, and counted $1,500 in five-, ten-, and twenty-dollar bills. He put the money in a brown paper bag, ordered a Scotch on the rocks, and waited. At 2 P.M. a squad car pulled up a few doors down the street from the bar. A police sergeant got out and entered the bar. The bar owner waved slightly. The sergeant then returned to the car. The numbers man also left the bar and entered a nearby barber shop, where the barber had been watching the scene from his window. The barber motioned to the numbers man that the coast was clear. The numbers man walked slowly from the barber shop to the squad car, dropped the bag into the back seat and returned to the bar. The bar owner then took a fifth of whiskey, put it in a bag, walked to the police car, reached across the sergeant who was on the right side of the front seat, and placed the bottle between him and the patrolman driver. The car drove off. Back at the bar the numbers banker ordered another Scotch and complained about the amount that the police were requiring him to pay. The payoff, he said, took place every two weeks, each time at a different location. "The sergeant makes more than I do," said the banker morosely.

Other bits and pieces of the story began to drift in. A numbers man showed his lawyer a payoff sheet for a couple of radio patrolmen. It showed that they received $2 each day at each of about thirty spots in their patrol area. "Do you realize," the gambler expostulated, "that these guys on a five-day week get $60 a day each, tax-free? That's $300 extra a week. At those prices they can't afford to go away on vacation!"

On July 6 a third grand jury was impaneled to sift through the complicated maze of evidence. A source close to the investigating team echoed what anonymous cops and bookies had told reporter Ted Poston in 1960: "It's big, plenty big. At this point we don't know how big it will get." Meanwhile, drinks were on the house at a number of bars where numbers play is known to occur. The reason was that, for the first time in many years, the police had not shown up to cart away their weekly bundles in brown paper bags.

CHAPTER NINE

The Tale That "Little Richie" Told

On the afternoon of January 14, 1960, Frank Ferlic, first assistant to Illinois State Attorney Benjamin Adamowski, and Paul Newey, Adamowski's chief investigator, appeared before a judge in Chicago and obtained the necessary search warrants.

That night was cold, wet, and windy. Outside the Conrad Hilton Hotel a group of police cars was lined up. Inside, forty carefully selected Chicago policemen, who had no idea of the nature of their assignment, were keeping an 8 P.M. appointment with Ferlic and Newey. The group consisted of high-ranking officers—supervising captains, captains, and lieutenants. When they were assembled, Ferlic and Newey handed them sealed envelopes which they were not to open until after they were back in their cars. Returning to their cars and opening the envelopes, the officers found themselves instructed to proceed to the homes of specified Chicago policemen. It was to be a simultaneous raid on eight different homes at 10:30 P.M. Once inside, the officers were to prevent any member of the raided households from making phone calls, search for certain specified stolen merchandise, and wait for the State attorney's men to come along with witnesses who would identify the stolen goods. The envelopes contained the search warrants.

One of the cars had an extra passenger, a slight, friendly, boyish-looking fellow named Richard C. Morrison, Jr. He was an erstwhile juvenile delinquent grown into an affable, weak, small-time burglar who loved to tell about his deeds. Fate had selected him for a key role in the history of police reform in the United States.

At 10:30 sharp, eight off-duty Chicago policemen heard knocks at their doors. Standing on their doorsteps were the raiding parties, who showed their warrants, entered, and began the search. In only one home did they come away empty-handed. It eventually took four police wagons to haul the television sets, outboard motors, electrical appliances, cameras, guns, radios, furniture, draperies, tires, antifreeze, automobile batteries, cigarette lighters, and other articles of stolen merchandise found in the other seven homes. After finishing their searches the raiders stood by while Morrison and certain recently burglarized Chicago merchants went from home to home, identifying stolen merchandise. The goods, with an estimated value of $20,000, were taken to Cook County Criminal Court Building where they filled up two whole rooms. (The total two-year haul of the police-burglary ring in Chicago was later estimated at $100,000.) The eight policemen—Murray Lemmon, Andrew Greer, George McKim, his brother Peter, Louis Corey, Thomas Bode, Edward Roper, and Anthony Torelli—were arrested and taken to a room in the Union League Club where they were questioned by Ferlic with five court stenographers present. Ferlic then turned the men over to their superiors, who took away their police stars and told them that they were "excused from duty." By the time it was all over and the last reporter had rushed to his city room with the sensational story it was dawn. It had been a long night in a city that has known many long nights of crime.

According to the records of the Chicago Crime Commission, Richard Morrison, the man responsible for it all, grew up in the Summerdale district of northern Chicago, where he attended Swift Elementary School and Senn High School. Reared by an indulgent grandmother after his parents were divorced, Morrison dropped out of high school after one year, and at the age of fifteen began stealing cars. In May 1953 while carrying a handsome assortment of burglary tools, he was stopped by detectives and arrested. He was sentenced to ten days in the county jail. A month later he was arrested again on the same charge and drew another ten-day term.

In 1954 he left Chicago. In December 1955 he was sentenced to nine months in Los Angeles county jail for burglary: he served four months and was granted probation for the other five. A year later he turned up in Las Vegas where he was jailed for a month as a prowler. Here he apparently developed a taste for gambling and he subsequently made frequent trips to Las Vegas to spend money that he had obtained from burglaries in Chicago.

Returning to Chicago in 1957, he picked up another four-month jail term for petty larceny. Soon after that he began to develop links with Summerdale policemen. What follows is a brief summary of parts of the tale that he subsequently told the State attorney's investigators, newspaper reporters, and the jury during the trial of the eight policemen.

Things began, he said, while he was working for a small pizza place in the Summerdale area. Soon after Morrison started, the proprietor made some special arrangements with the Summerdale police. Delivery trucks were having difficulty parking close enough while making their deliveries, especially during the rush hours. When they double-parked they promptly received tickets. Morrison's boss knew how to solve the problem; he invited the policemen detailed to the area to come in and eat free of charge. The ticketing stopped. Before long Morrison had become acquainted with a number of policemen.

One day Morrison was walking down Berwyn Avenue near the pizza place when a policeman, Murray Lemmon, walked out of a corner saloon. He and Morrison had met at the pizza restaurant. Lemmon waved a greeting and said, "Well, if it isn't the little burglar Richie."

"Hi, Murray, how are things with you?" Morrison replied.

"Well, they would be a little better if you would cut us guys in on some of your jobs," Lemmon said confidingly. "You know Pete McKim and some of the other fellows, and we'd go along with the show. After all, we like nice things too!"

After that a number of policemen renewed the none-too-subtle hints. Peter McKim told him that Andrew Greer wanted to know when Morrison was going to steal some golf clubs for Greer. After about a month of such queries, Morrison got drunk one night and drove up to the Evanston area to look for some golf clubs. He began checking the rear seats of cars and eventually came upon a station wagon with golf clubs inside. He started to break into the car, but Evanston police hailed him. Morrison jumped into his car and roared away. The pursuing policemen fired a number of shots, one of which punctured a tire. Morrison abandoned the car and escaped, but the car was traced to his home. He was arrested and in February 1959 was convicted in criminal court of auto looting. Morrison's lawyer made a motion for a new trial, and subsequently all proceedings against him were dropped. He was a state's evidence witness in the trial of the cop-burglars.

After this episode Morrison began to work with the policemen of the Summerdale district in performing burglaries. He paid the policemen in cash and stolen goods, either for active cooperation in the burglaries, or their willingness to drop or soft-pedal investigations of crimes in which he was involved. At first, Morrison said, the police acted principally as lookouts while he committed burglaries. They would cruise around the block, keep away other policemen, and intercept private watchmen and detain them with conversation long enough for Morrison to complete his work.

Soon, Morrison and his police friends were meeting regularly in a restaurant at 1 A.M. and planning burglaries. One night they decided to rob a music store at Balmoral and Clark Streets. Morrison broke into the store. Meanwhile policeman Murray Lemmon was at the Summerdale station. He heard a radio call being sent out to prowl cars that a burglary was in process at the store. Lemmon jumped into squad car 207 (the jury was impressed by Morrison's detailed knowledge of Summerdale police equipment and his ability to cite by number the squad cars used in specific cases), blocked off the street on which the music store was located, and flashed his spotlight into the store window. Morrison, who had already looted the cash drawer, slipped out of the store and met in the back alley with other policemen who had been serving as lookouts. When a detective bureau car arrived half a minute later Lemmon flagged it down and conferred with its occupants. Morrison vaulted over a fence, jumped into his car, and got away without difficulty. Morrison says that, in appreciation for Lemmon's swift help on this occasion, he gave him all the money that he had stolen from the cash drawer, amounting to several hundred dollars.

On another occasion Morrison said that policemen involved with him in looting a food store nearly shot a private watchman. Morrison and five officers drove to the store in car 207. While the policemen waited, Morrison jimmied the door. The cops entered and began hauling away all the food they could carry. Morrison, realizing that nobody was in the car listening to the radio, left the store and sat in the car, while the policemen shuttled back and forth from the store, filling it up with bacon, hams, and other foodstuffs.

Suddenly another car, driven by an employee of a private watchman agency, pulled up nearby. Morrison realized that if he and all the stolen merchandise were seen in the squad car the game would be up. He promptly drove off in the squad car. When he returned a few minutes later the five policemen were still there. Morrison explained his quick, unscheduled departure. "We almost had a heart attack ourselves," one of the policemen told him. "We had our guns on him. We all laid low in the store. But this guy was checking the door of a place next door. He must have missed us completely. We might have had to drop him if he had seen us." After this incident his police friends offered to lend Morrison a uniform to wear when accompanying the police on burglaries. Morrison declined it, saying that it was too much trouble changing back and forth, and that it was better and easier just to stay out of sight.

After Morrison had been working with the police in

performing burglaries for about a year, he was burglariz-
ing a store on Lawrence Avenue one night when some
shots were fired at him. Morrison assumed that they were
fired by one of his alleged police friends, because he now
knew so much and could incriminate so many policemen.
On subsequent jobs he requested that the lookout services
be performed by certain policemen, whom Morrison privately believed to be the most reliable.

Soon thereafter the police asked him to crack open a meat
market. Morrison agreed, selecting the policeman who
would be the lookout. This policeman stayed outside on a
three-wheel motorcycle while Morrison entered and picked
up $1,300 in cash from the register. He also worked on
the safe but found that he could not open it without blowing it, and decided not to make the noise. As he walked
out he told the policeman-lookout, "The door's open. You
can round up the guys and bring them in."

Morrison went down an alley and climbed up on a
garage roof to watch the show. The policeman apparently
called in nearly every available vehicle in the district, including all the three-wheel motorcycles, the local patrolling
squad car, and a paddy wagon. They turned on their lights
and loaded up all the vehicles, practically cleaning out
the meat market. For quite a few days thereafter Morrison had steaks for breakfast at the homes of his policemen friends.

Next, Morrison and the policemen looted a store selling
appliances and auto supplies. This time he came a crop-
per. A few days later two detectives who were not involved
in the burglary ring found some spark plugs in Morrison's
car that had been listed as part of the loot. The detectives
arrested him, took him to the station house, and put him
in the lock-up. At the time, most of the loot from this

burglary was still in Morrison's house, since he had not yet divided it up with his policemen allies. But as soon as Morrison was in the lock-up, several of his buddies showed up, and Morrison gave them the keys to his apartment. Jumping into notorious squad car 207, the policemen rushed to Morrison's apartment and removed all the stolen goods, including about $5,000 worth of radio and television sets. The cops divided the loot and held it in their own homes.

Morrison was soon out, and promptly got busy on more burglaries. The next victim was an auto-supply store. The job was planned by Morrison and the police. A perplexity arose when, arriving at the premises, they found a car double-parked by the loading dock at the rear of the store. Not knowing whether the owner might come down to drive the car away at an embarrassing moment, Morrison and the cops waited a couple of hours. Nothing happened. Then a squad car drove by, driven by one of the conspirator cops. Morrison explained the problem to the driver. The squad car obligingly pushed the car out onto Broadway. "To hell with the guy," said the driver of the police cruiser. After that, while Morrison looted the place, the police car circled around the block every few minutes, and sent away two or three watchmen of the private service patrol.

As Morrison's string of successful burglaries increased, policemen vied for his services to the point of chasing each other in squad cars. At the trial Morrison told the jury that one night in November, 1958, he was in a squad car with Murray Lemmon and Peter McKim. They were cruising on Broadway near Balmoral about 11 P.M. when they encountered another squad car with Thomas Bode and Louis Corey coming in the opposite direction. "Pete Mc-

Kim said to Murray Lemmon that Bode and Corey were making a U-turn and coming after us," Morrison related. "They told me to get in the back seat and down on the floor so they [Bode and Corey] wouldn't see me if they hadn't seen me already. Then Murray Lemmon drove east on Balmoral and over some sidewalks and down some alleys with this other car chasing us. Lemmon went into Winthrop [a one-way street] the wrong way off Foster. As he stopped I jumped out of the car and rolled under a nearby parked automobile."

The other squad car pulled up and screeched to a halt. As he lay under the car, Morrison said, he heard Bode say to Lemmon and McKim, "What's going on, are you playing games tonight?" "No, why?" Lemmon replied. "I thought I saw little Richie with you," Bode said suspiciously. Either Lemmon or McKim—Morrison isn't sure which—replied to Bode, "You must be seeing things." The four cops talked together briefly and they parted, with Bode commenting, "If there's anything going on tonight, we'd like to get into it."

The burglary ring continued to flourish, with the police continuing to give Morrison efficient help. Once when Morrison was cutting a hole in the roof of a tire store he was observed by a neighborhood resident who called the police. A squad car was dispatched by radio. The message was picked up by the cops in the squad car who were covering Morrison's burglary. They warned him to lie flat on the roof. When other officers arrived in another car to investigate they were told by the cops on the scene that their presence was not needed since they would handle the complaint. The other squad car drove away, the cops gave Morrison the all-clear sign, and he completed the job.

Most of the burglaries were committed with the help of policemen who were on duty and in uniform. Morrison said that, for convenience, his policemen friends carried burglary tools in the squad car while they were on duty. One patrolman, however, who had previously owned a tavern on North Sheridan Road, suggested to Morrison that they break into the place on the officer's day off, to avoid the necessity of sharing the loot with the other cops. Morrison agreed. The burglary netted fifteen cases of liquor and a set of carpentry tools.

Morrison, meanwhile, also became involved in passing counterfeit money. In December 1958 an acquaintance in the Chicago underworld gave him a bundle of counterfeit hundred-dollar bills to cash. Morrison approached his police friends to see if they would be willing to help him pass the counterfeit money, but found that the officers "didn't want to take hundreds" because such large bills were too risky to pass. They were willing to accept twenty-dollar bills, according to Morrison, but he didn't have any. However, he had at least one success. A Chicago police officer who had just joined the force and was still on a probationary status was later discharged because of his association with Morrison and for passing a one-hundred-dollar counterfeit bill. Morrison left Chicago to pass the rest of the money, which angered his policemen friends. They complained that "I wasn't giving them any of my time."

The burglary rate in the Summerdale district began to soar. Some insurance companies suffered losses up to 288 percent of the premiums received and quit writing insurance in the area. The manager of an auto-supply store had his place burglarized four times in eighteen months. On three of these occasions a huge section of a plate-glass window right on the street had been cut away to facilitate the carting out of heavy, bulky items. After the scandal broke, the store manager said, "Those guys broke into this store four times and cleaned it out—guns, television sets, appliances, everything that wasn't nailed down. Then I'll be a dirty son of a gun if one of them didn't come around at Christmastime and ask for a handout!"

Morrison himself later discovered that the police had been playing a double game with him too. Sometimes, after he had pulled a job with the cooperation or connivance of Summerdale policemen, these same policemen would tip off detectives that Morrison had been implicated. Morrison then found it necessary to pay off the detectives to have the investigation dropped. The detectives, for their part, would kick back a portion of Morrison's payment to the policemen who had tipped them off.

On July 30, 1959, Morrison was arrested in a burglary investigation. Under questioning he proved to be astonishingly cooperative, admitting many burglaries. He told reporters, "I've done 150 jobs in the last six months and picked up about $100,000. Also I've passed out $180,000 worth of phony dough. I guess I'm all through, now."

Within a few days he began to spill the beans about his link to the Summerdale cops. However, he found it remarkably difficult to find anyone who would listen to him.

Meanwhile, Morrison was charged on six counts of burglary. During the proceedings, he suddenly blurted out, "I would like to see State Attorney Adamowski before these cases even start, your honor, because there's a few things that aren't squared off here in these cases. It's a matter of quite a few police officers involved here. They have been messing around and around." He was tried, sentenced, and taken to jail.

In jail he was visited by State attorney aides Frank Ferlic and Paul Newey. They listened to his story and began a quiet investigation. This led to the raid on the homes of the eight policemen on January 14, 1960.

The scandal burgeoned as Morrison reeled off more accusations, leading to more arrests. Two hundred and twenty-nine Summerdale policemen were given lie-detector tests. Later it was discovered that some cops took tranquilizers before submitting to the tests in order to render the findings uncertain.

A whirlwind of other revelations and accusations, unrelated to Morrison's tale, soon followed. The Chicago Crime Commission reported that policeman Francis Meagher, while performing off-duty work as a watchman for a store from April to September 1959, had been busy looting the place. When caught, Meagher implicated a fellow officer, Charles Eaton, and the two made nominal restitution of $700. At first the firm did not press charges because it "didn't want to get on the wrong side of the police force." During the employment of Meagher, other officers were permitted to enter the store, steal merchandise, and haul it away in squad cars.

Many citizens chimed in by relaying long-smoldering accusations against the police to Chicago newspapers. One ex-policeman, writing to the Chicago *Tribune* under his own signature, provided a large dossier of information, including names, dates, and places, describing links between police and crime in Chicago. Among his accusations:

¶ A high-ranking police official permitted the city's largest continuing dice game to operate in his district, on orders from a Democratic ward committeeman. The police official received a rake-off from both gambling and vice.

¶ Thirty-nine gambling operations flourished on a wide open basis in another police district under the same official. Two bagmen came by for regular rake-offs, one for the police official and one for the ward committeeman.

¶ Another high police officer was part owner of a hotel where prostitution flourished. A patrolman was maintained on duty at all times. His job was to see that no arrests were made and that no customer failed to pay for services rendered.

¶ A police official assigned to "investigate" several men on vice shakedown charges had actually been using these same men as his personal collectors from vice joints throughout the city. Nothing came of the investigation.

¶ A high police officer in a supervisory position was sometimes drunk at roll calls that he conducted himself. This official hid his squad car while spending time with hoodlums and prostitutes.

¶ A police captain's nephew acted as bagman for his uncle and several other captains. The captain and his nephew were constantly in the company of top syndicate hoodlums.

¶ A prominent Chicago politician and officeholder made a trip to Arizona to get a large sum of money put up by the crime syndicate to secure the promotion of a certain police lieutenant to the rank of captain.

After receiving this letter, the *Tribune* sent reporters to interview a number of police commanders, lieutenants, and veteran detectives. Their response was bitter and unanimous. "Politicians wield the clout [influence] in the department like a club," said one. A chief of detectives said that sponsorship of a Democratic politician was essential before a policeman could be transferred to the detective bureau. "Appointment of patrolmen to the rank of detective became a part of the Democratic city administration's political patronage," he said. "Sponsorship of a committeeman, an alderman, or a party organization chief of some kind was mandatory before a patrolman could make the $600-a-year jump in salary that goes with a detective rating."

"I can't make a detective or dump him," a captain said, "and thus I have no control over my own men. They know it. A man doesn't have to give a damn about me. He listens to the politician who helped him get his rank."

In February 1960 a special grand jury was called to probe the mess. In March it indicted Morrison and the eight Summerdale policemen caught in the January 14 raids. (The state later dropped its proceedings against Morrison.) All eight policemen were convicted of conspiracy to burglarize and to conceal stolen property. Roper accepted and served his sentence of six months in jail and a $1,000 fine. The others appealed their convictions; at the time of this writing the appeals are still pending.

In March the grand jury also indicted policemen Samuel Lucas and Paul Hyde on charges of conspiracy to obstruct justice. The jury stated that they had removed from police custody a camera stolen by Morrison and had substituted another in order to damage the state's case against Morrison. Both were convicted.

When the scandal broke in January 1960 with the raids on the eight policemen's homes, the public reacted with shock and anger. Mayor Richard Daley cut a Florida vacation short and hurried back to the city. On January 23 he announced that Police Commissioner Timothy O'Connor was resigning. O'Connor's personal integrity was acknowledged by everyone. "O'Connor, who had headed the department since 1950, was a man of unimpeachable integrity," the Chicago Crime Commission stated in its 1960 report. "He had been responsible for many improvements in the department and was one of Chicago's better Commissioners of Police. Nevertheless, the scandal broke during his regime because of fundamental weaknesses present in the organizational structure of the department as well as the philosophy that had always governed its administration. Commissioner O'Connor had been virtually powerless to eliminate these basic weaknesses. A complete reorganization of the department was an absolute necessity."

At the same press conference, Mayor Daley announced that he was appointing a five-man civilian committee "to select the best qualified available man in the nation to serve as head of the Chicago Police Department and to make policy recommendations for its reorganization."

Named to the committee were: Orlando W. Wilson, dean of the School of Criminology at the University of California and an internationally known authority on modern police methods; Franklin M. Kreml, director of Northwestern University Transportation Center; Paul W. Goodrich, president of the Chicago Association of Commerce and Industry; William L. McFetridge, president of the Building Service Employees International Union and a vice president of AFL-CIO; and Virgil W. Peterson, operating director of the Chicago Crime Commission and a famous authority on crime.

Public interest and speculation ran high as the committee began its work. The group considered, and eliminated without interview, fifty-three applicants and nominees. It interviewed twenty-four members of the Chicago Police Department, three other residents of Chicago, and ten persons residing outside Illinois.

As the deliberations continued, the other four members of the committee became increasingly convinced that the best man for the job was the man who was serving as president of the committee, Orlando W. Wilson. Mr. Kreml, as vice-chairman of the committee, conferred with the other members and finally approached Wilson on the subject. When he was approached by the committee to take the job, Wilson held a $14,700-a-year post at the University of California, had already done a big stint of public service, and had achieved high recognition in his field. Nearing sixty, he would have retired the following July 1 with a comfortable pension. He and his wife were already house-hunting in Hawaii.

From 1921 to 1925 he had been a patrolman in Berkeley, California. After serving as chief of police of Fullerton, California, for a few months in 1925, he became a private investigator for a few years, then was appointed chief of police in Wichita, Kansas, a position he held from 1928 to 1939. In 1939 he became professor of police administration in a pioneer program launched by the University of California. In World War II he joined the Army, coming out as a colonel with the Bronze Star and Legion of Merit for service in Europe. He returned to the California faculty and became dean of the university's School of Criminology in 1950. In the 1950's he wrote a standard text on modern police procedures and directed reorganization surveys in a number of towns and cities.

Taken by surprise at the committee's approach, Wilson told them that if they wished to consider him he would first have to resign from the body. The other committee mem-mers told him that they indeed want to consider him, and he therefore resigned. The committee spent all day Sunday, January 22, talking with Wilson. Late in the afternoon, after calling his wife, he said yes. The committee immediately reported to Mayor Daley its belief that Wilson was the man for the job. Mayor Daley acted immediately; on Monday he called a press conference and introduced the astonished reporters to the new superintendent of police for the city of Chicago, Orlando W. Wilson.

Wilson met the swarming reporters with a smile and with carefully chosen words: "I consider this the greatest challenge in law enforcement today. Progress will be of a necessity made slowly, and no capricious actions will be undertaken." Mayor Daley told the press that the riot act had gone out from his office: no more political hands on the police. "I have given Professor Wilson my assurance that no influences upon the police department will be used by anyone," Daley said in measured tones.

The people of Chicago reacted with interest, curiosity, and a combination of cautious hope and skepticism, understandable in a city in which 998 hoodlums had been shot down in the streets since 1919 and only two of the murders had been solved. John Swaagman, 7127 South Peoria Street, a grocer, probably summed up the city's mood: "You don't know who you can trust now. I hope he can do the job."

CHAPTER TEN

"Out of Adversity"— The Chicago Reform

The reform of the Chicago Police Department is a subject for a book in itself. And, in fact, it will be at least partially covered in a scholarly book. In the summer of 1964, Herman Goldstein, Superintendent Wilson's thirty-two-year-old executive assistant, received a Ford Foundation grant to write a book on modern police procedures in metropolitan areas. Goldstein expects to draw heavily on his four years' experience as a top official in the Chicago reform administration in writing the book.

When Superintendent Wilson was officially sworn in on March 2, 1960, as Chicago's first civilian police head (the title was changed from commissioner to superintendent of police), he faced a fantastic job. Prior to his arrival, there had never been a genuine reorganization of the police department in Chicago's entire history. "The Chicago force was badly equipped and poorly organized—a regular Smithsonian Institution of law enforcement," says George W. O'Connor, a consultant in the field service division in the International Association of Chiefs of Police. "Today, it is probably the best-equipped, best-administered police force in the United States."

When he took office Wilson announced that his two objectives were to eliminate corruption from the force and to turn it into the nation's best crime-fighting and law-enforcement agency. The two objectives were, of course, interrelated. Corruption thrives on poor supervision, improper administration, and low morale. Conversely, the feeling of being part of a "crack outfit" has a strong positive effect on morale and is a deterrent to corruption, which is felt to be a sabotage of the common effort. Also, the very act of creating a more efficient crime-fighting force causes some weaker men to drop out. "Wilson raised the level of what was expected from each man," O'Connor says.

Wilson did almost no firing, but within four years there had been a 25 percent changeover in personnel. In 1959, the last year of the old administration, 131 policemen who were eligible for pensions resigned and an additional 131 resigned without pensions from the 13,000-man force. In 1960 the figures rose to 334 and 229 respectively. In subsequent years they dropped sharply, with the number of those resigning without pensions falling below the 1959 level.

When Wilson began he had two indispensable assets, all-too-rare when cities bring in reform police administrations. First, Mayor Daley assured him that he would brook no political interference with any reforms that Wilson thought necessary. The mayor, one of the most able and powerful of modern city executives, made sure that this word reached down into the rank and file of the Chicago Democratic political organization, and made it clear that the pronouncement was not window dressing. Principal targets of the mayor's pronouncement were the city aldermen and the committeemen in Chicago's fifty wards, who had long been accustomed to using the police department for political rewards and patronage. A policeman who had political influence could expect promotion and good assignments. Without it he could often expect to spend eight hours a day guarding a building. During an investigation of a bribery scandal that took place shortly before Wilson's arrival, Mathias Bauler, a saloonkeeper and aldermen of the forty-third ward, said, "Chicago ain't ready for reform!" But public anger and chagrin at the Summerdale police burglary ring had given Daley the leverage he needed, and he used it resolutely. ("People can *grasp* this one," a Chicago businessman said grimly to a *New York Times* reporter.)

Underlining his own intention to retain political independence, Superintendent Wilson, as one of his first official acts, moved his office out of City Hall, where it had been from time immemorial, and into the police headquarters building.

The second important step made by Mayor Daley was to assure Superintendent Wilson that police budget requests would be backed to the hilt. Wilson was to tailor his program to meet the need, not to meet political expediency. Daley assured him that the full power of the mayor's office would be used to see that Wilson got the money.

During his first week in office Superintendent Wilson held two mass meetings in which he spoke to the entire force. He told them that he planned big changes but that every man who performed his duty could be sure that his job as a policeman was secure. To Chicago citizens he addressed a special plea to discontinue a practice that had become all but universal in the city. Drivers made a practice of keeping a five-dollar bill clipped to their licenses. When stopped by a policeman for a traffic violation, the driver would hand the policeman the license with the five dollars attached. The policeman would glance at the license, remove the five dollars, pocket it, return the license, and wave the driver on. Wilson pointed out that drivers who paid five dollars for this type of "protection" were laying the foundation for the purchase of larger "protection" by criminals. Simultaneously with his plea, Wilson gave his force an order that had never before been issued by the Chicago Police Department. Any citizen who offered a policeman a bribe was to be immediately arrested. As we shall see in the next chapter, these two actions, along with the establishment of the internal investigation division shortly thereafter, had a drastic impact.

Wilson moved swiftly into a three-part program: full administrative reorganization; introduction of new police techniques; modernization of plant and equipment. He brought in several nationally known experts in law enforcement and public administration as top aides, and retained a group of outside experts on a consulting basis in the fields of police communications, crime statistics, research and planning, police training, youth work, and psychiatry. By the end of 1960 a substantial revolution was under way.

By 1964 the department had almost been born anew in terms of its equipment and facilities. "I wish you had seen this headquarters building four years ago," Superintendent Wilson said to me in 1964. "You couldn't imagine a more dreary and miserable place to work. Law-enforcement officers do indispensable work and their working environment should reflect the importance of their task." Beginning in 1961 the old, gray thirteen-story police headquarters building was practically stripped to its steel skeleton, and a new, functional building with a four-story annex, rose in its place. Completed at a cost of $4 million, the new headquarters was dedicated by Mayor Daley in 1963. One feature of the renovated building is the use of glass partitions that enable the public to view all major facilities of the department. Headsets on the wall provide tape-recorded descriptions of the work of each department in operation. The new headquarters has become a favorite showcase for both Chicago residents and tourists. It seems to symbolize the difference between the old and the new. "Out of adversity," said Mayor Daley in dedicating the building, "we have built a modern and efficient police force."

From 1960 to 1964 the department's squad car strength grew from 515 to more than 1,200. The old three-wheel motorcycles have been retired from general patrol work. These machines had the dubious double distinction of costing, with their radio equipment, more than squad cars, and being universally hated by the men who rode them. More than one officer in the sidecar was killed or injured while trying to curb a drunken driver, and when it comes to gunfire—something that can always happen—the man in the "bathtub" is a sitting duck.

From the top to the bottom of the department, modern machines and equipment were installed. "I'd been using the same typewriter since 1936," said a veteran captain. "Now I've got a new one. I can hardly believe it!" On a larger scale, the communications equipment and computers installed by the Chicago department are completely new departures in police work anywhere. On the basis of Chicago's successful use of high-speed computers in police operations, similar setups have been ordered by the New York City Police Department and by Scotland Yard.

The communications center, created and built at a cost

of $2 million, is perhaps the most revolutionary achievement of the Wilson administration. For a long time, residents of large cities have been accustomed to getting service from the fire department within one or two minutes after placing their calls. By contrast, police service has been capricious and slow, even in emergencies in which life may be at stake. Chicago was no exception. Commissioner Wilson sought to create a system that would bring every citizen of Chicago within three minutes' reach of police help. He and his consultants from the International Association of Chiefs of Police created a system that has achieved the goal. In fact, the police car sometimes arrives while the citizen is still on the telephone talking to police headquarters.

In Chicago's old system, when a call came in for police help, a girl operator would answer, write down the complaint on a slip of paper and place the slip on a moving belt to the dispatch room. There it was given to one of four dispatchers, who put out the radio call. All the dispatcher knew about the complaint was the information written on the slip of paper by the telephone girl. He had no clear idea of the urgency of the call, and he could not get in touch with the caller to ask questions or obtain clarification. Further difficulty was created because there were only two radio frequencies on which calls were transmitted. During peak hours a backlog of as many as one hundred calls would pile up. Sometimes it was even necessary to pass on calls received in the central complaint room to district stations by telephone. As a result, it used to take up to six hours between the time a citizen called the police and the arrival of a squad car on the scene.

In the new communications center, dispatchers sit at thirty-six consoles, each of which has a large, lighted map of Chicago. The dispatchers, who are policemen, take calls directly from the public. The city is divided into eight communications zones, each zone being watched over by three console operators. Each zone comprises several telephone exchanges. A telephone call from a given exchange is automatically routed to a console operator covering the zone of the caller's exchange. The illuminated maps on each console have lights showing the patrol cars available for service in the zone that the dispatcher is covering.

When a call comes in, the console operator time-stamps an IBM card, writes the complaint on it, and immediately radios one of the available cars. If desirable, he can keep the complainant on the phone and get further information from him at the same time that he is talking to the squad car on his microphone. As soon as the squad car has the report and is rushing to the scene, the console operator inserts the IBM card into a slot in the console, causing that car's light to disappear from the screen. The light goes back on as soon as the car has completed the mission and is ready for further assignment. Six consoles are available for handling an overflow of any zone. The remaining two of the thirty-six are for use by the communications center's supervisor, who acts as a field general.

This system, along with the heavy reinforcement in the number of patrol cars and reduction in the size of the patrol area of each car, has achieved Wilson's goal of putting every citizen within three minutes' reach of police help. Actually, three minutes is an unusually long time for a citizen to wait; the police car usually arrives within a minute. The record is seven seconds.

In the old system, the patrolman, after responding to a complaint, would subsequently go to his district station house and peck out a report on an antediluvian typewriter.

This not only took the patrolman off his beat for substantial periods of time, but resulted in laconic, sketchy reports, with essential details missing. Now, as soon as he has finished an assignment, the patrolman picks up a telephone, dials a number, and is immediately connected with a dictating machine in police headquarters. He dictates a report right over the phone, giving a full, complete record of the circumstances he found and the action he took, within seconds or minutes after he has completed the assignment. When he puts down the phone he returns to his squad car and is immediately ready for further assignments. In the dictation room at headquarters, three shifts of stenographers are on duty twenty-four hours a day; reports from the policemen on the beat are typed in a number of copies within minutes after they are received.

Meanwhile, the IBM card filled out by the dispatcher is passed on to a key-punch operator, who punches out information cards on the basis of the facts on the dispatcher's card. This information goes into daily, weekly, and monthly statistical reports, giving the superintendent and his aides a detailed picture of patterns of crime in the city. It is assembled, broken down and stored by high-speed computers.

The planning division studies this information carefully. Patterns for assigning men to beats on the basis of crime incidence, varying needs at different times of day, and seasonal variations, are determined from the statistics. Many traditional police controversies have been settled by proper use of the data. For example, the amount and type of crime and arrests in each area determines whether one or two officers are assigned to squad cars. Extensive use of one-man patrol cars is now being made in many areas so that the size of each squad car's beat can be reduced and patrol coverage can be intensified with existing manpower. The computers have been put to hundreds of other uses. Daily attendance records are now prepared by computer, saving $250,000 a year in man-hours previously expended in typing attendance reports each day, on each watch, in each payroll unit.

A similar search for efficiency has brought about hundreds of procedural changes at all levels. Polaroid cameras photograph prisoners at district station houses, eliminating the former practice of transporting prisoners to headquarters. Preventive maintenance of vehicles is performed on the midnight watch, with a jockey system being used to transfer cars to the garage while officers on patrol use replacement vehicles from a motor pool. This has virtually eliminated the formerly frequent occasions when a police officer was unable to patrol his beat for lack of a car.

While introducing new methods and techniques, Superintendent Wilson brought about a complete administrative reorganization. Within the superintendent's office are five divisions: finance, management analysis, planning, personnel, public information. The main body of the force is divided into three large bureaus, the bureau of staff services, the bureau of field services, and the bureau of inspectional services, each under a deputy superintendent reporting to Wilson. Divisions under staff services include the crime laboratory, records and communications, training, and maintenance. The bureau of field services includes the patrol division, traffic division, detective division, and youth division. The bureau of inspectional services includes the intelligence division, the inspection division, the vice control division, and the internal investigation division (the latter division, dealing directly with problems of corruption within the department, is the subject of the next chapter).

This setup involved the creation of new groups, consolidation of others, and the shuffling and reorganization of many other functions. During the first year 260 men were shifted or transferred. New ranks were created and old ones abolished. Men slated for consideration for top posts in the department were carefully screened and were given day-long interviews by a management consulting firm retained by the department. At the top levels Wilson created a number of "exempt positions"—positions that could be filled by officers of, say, the rank of captain, but which brought salaries substantially higher than that received by captains. These men are responsible to the superintendent and hold their "exempt" status at his pleasure. It need not be added that their loyalty to the goals of his program has been high.

The way up was opened for merit, and some men got big promotions. Sgt. William Duffy was promoted from desk sergeant to director of the intelligence division; his salary went up from $6,888 to $12,380. Captain Joseph Morris became head of the bureau of inspectional services, one of the three main divisions of the force. From 1952 to 1956 Captain Morris had headed a special intelligence unit combating organized crime. "The unit performed outstanding work in checking on Chicago's overlords of crime, in the development and coordination of information relating to the city's leading criminals and racketeering elements, as well as their associates in the professional, business and political worlds," says Virgil Peterson, operating director of the Chicago Crime Commission. The unit apparently did its work too well; it was disbanded under political pressure in 1956. Under Wilson, Captain Morris' abilities were put back to use.

Wilson directed major attention to the detective bureau. The bureau had a long list of major, unsolved crimes when Wilson took over. He invited Stanley Schrotel, head of the Cincinnati force, and subsequently a president of the International Association of Chiefs of Police, to come in and survey the bureau. After the survey and after extended study and consideration, a basic change was made. Detectives were taken out of the twenty-one district stations and transferred to six area headquarters where they worked under the direct command of the chief of detectives. Detective teams were broken up, and detectives worked alone unless more than one was assigned to a case. Detectives had previously handled all details of major crimes, but now they rarely rush to the scene of felonies. Uniformed policemen or patrol officers conduct detailed preliminary investigations, including interviews with complainants and witnesses. They submit their field reports to the detective bureau, which then follows up on the crime. The shift was designed to make maximum use of the special training and special skills of both patrolmen and detectives. The change broke up old alliances, old friendships, and old patterns of work, and it met with some grumbling and resistance. But early opponents of the plan now concede that it has made the detective bureau vastly more effective.

The chain of command has been tightened in the force. The responsibilities of each patrolman, sergeant, and officer have been specified. Commanding officers are now held fully responsible both for the performance of their own duties and for the failure of those under them to carry out their functions. This system entailed a need for more supervisory personnel and has opened the channels of advancement. When Wilson became superintendent in 1960 he found that no examinations had been given for advancement at some levels for thirteen years. Under normal promotional policies, many men would have been lieutenants and a few would have been captains if they had been allowed to take regularly scheduled exams. Morale had suffered severely.

Under Wilson, examinations for sergeant were promptly given, and examinations for promotions to lieutenant and captain followed. A second examination for sergeant and lieutenant has since been held and the department plans to schedule promotional examinations every two years. Between March 1960 and January 1964, 873 men were promoted to sergeant, 226 to lieutenant, and 94 to captain. The ratio between the number of patrolmen and their immediate superiors has been sharply reduced. In the patrol division all sergeants have been supplied with motor vehicles and assigned specific beats for direct supervision. In this and all other divisions, supervisors are expected to correct faults and improve performance and productivity.

Along with more opportunity for advancement, salaries have been going up for all policemen in all grades. In the period 1960 to 1964, raises for patrolmen have totaled 15 percent, plus the establishment of a $120-a-year uniform allowance. The time for reaching the maximum salary level for patrolmen has been cut from forty-eight to forty-two months. Selection for the rank of detective is now a prerogative of the superintendent of police rather than the civil service board. The civil service board had originally tried to keep municipal employment isolated from politics, but appointments to the board were political and over the years politics inevitably crept into some of its actions and decisions. Competitive examinations for detective are now administered by the department itself. Testing techniques have been greatly refined—motion pictures of crime scenes serve as the basis for a portion of the examination. Grading is performed by machine immediately after the test, while the examinees are present, and grades are posted within hours after the exams.

As part of the administrative reorganization, patrol districts in the city were realigned and district stations were reduced in number from thirty-eight to twenty-one, bringing about more efficient service and also making it possible to reassign to street duty 180 officers previously tied up in routine tasks in the now-abandoned district stations. In other steps to make more effective use of available manpower, scores of officers have been withdrawn from duties which do not require the specific attention of a policeman, and hundreds have been returned to field service from special details. A total of 478 additional civilian crossing guards have been appointed to help schoolchildren across busy intersections, freeing policemen from this duty. Clerical tasks at district stations and at headquarters are performed by a staff of civilian employees which has been increased by more than 850 persons. Fifty college students are hired each summer to conduct a dog-license check previously performed by police officers. Police cadets who are a part of the department's training program are assigned to police headquarters and help to relieve regular policemen from routine functions.

The cadet program is part of greatly changed patterns of recruitment, selection, and training. The department has sought more applicants while sharply raising selection standards and the standards and quality of training. Superintendent Wilson had hoped to be able to do nationwide recruiting for the Chicago department, but thus far the city council has been willing to expand the recruiting area only from Chicago to all of Cook County, in which Chicago is located. Within this area all facilities of mass communication are employed to reach possible applicants. Recruiting campaigns are conducted in high schools and colleges. Recruiting officers have been stationed at strategic locations in the city and county. Contests are held among policemen on the force for recruiting the largest number of men. Entrance examinations are held several times a year. "The greatest factor in getting good men is the prestige of the service," says Superintendent Wilson, and adds, "Our prestige is growing."

The number of applicants has sharply increased, making it possible to put higher selection standards into effect. Screening has been tightened, intensive background checks of all candidates are conducted, and psychological testing and psychiatric evaluation are used. Indicative of the high standards is the fact that a recent examination was taken by 2,183 applicants, of whom only 141 were certified as eligible for appointment—one out of every fifteen who applied.

The police cadet program enables qualified high school graduates to begin their law-enforcement careers while attending college. They wear cadets' uniforms and work with the force at specified hours and during the summer months. They are eligible to take the examination for patrolman when they reach the age of twenty-one.

Training programs for successful applicants to the force have been strengthened and in-service training has been greatly expanded. The police Training Division Library, a new branch of the Municipal Reference Library, has one of the country's most comprehensive collections of materials on police and criminology. Policemen may use intradepartmental mail to borrow and return books. Business is brisk. The training division has also launched a correspondence course in criminal investigation. The course requires 160 hours of study, and is conducted through the intradepartmental mail. Over 600 members of the department have so far completed the course. A course in criminal law has now been started, and will soon be followed by others.

The department adjusts the work schedule of any member who wishes to study at the college level. With department cooperation, the Chicago branch of the University of Illinois has established a program in police science. The department has been working closely with the university to develop the program, and hopes that eventually the university will offer a degree in the field. Plans are now in the making for a program at the University of Illinois in the administration of criminal justice, leading to bachelor's, master's and doctorate degrees. As early as 1961 Superintendent Wilson proposed a four-year college course for Chicago policemen, and he eventually expects to see this goal realized.

The new procedures have carried the department a long way from selection procedures of the recent past which were, in the gentle word of the IACP's George O'Connor, "uninformed." One man joined the force on August 16, 1957. Six years earlier he had been brought in to boys' court and placed under supervision for six months for participating in the theft of $15,000 worth of television tubes. He was at that time an employee of an electronics company, and was one of fifteen employees involved in the theft. When he applied for a position on the police force the department checked his employment record and learned from the company of the theft. He was nevertheless appointed to the force.

With these immense changes the Chicago police force

has become a new organization. Better performance, better morale, more prestige, and community interest in the effort to stamp out the image of Chicago police corruption, are among the results. The effort is also paying off in the ultimate goal of police—reduction of crime. During the first year of Superintendent Wilson's administration there was an apparent increase in the Chicago crime rate, as is usually the case when reform administrations are brought into police departments. It also partly reflects the nationwide rise in the crime rate which has been continuing over many years. The city whose crime rate does *not* increase has actually achieved something simply in resisting the national trend.

After the first year of the new regime, Chicago's crime rate stabilized and then began to drop. In 1963, while major offenses were increasing 10 percent on the nationwide level, they decreased by 8.6 percent in Chicago. The largest reductions occurred in the overall category of crimes against persons and robberies, which were reduced by 16.5 percent. Serious assaults were down 26.5 percent, rapes 30 percent, robberies 8.2 percent, homicides 8 percent, burglaries 7.8 percent.

Commissioner Wilson, who has received the greatest recognition of his career for the reorganization of the Chicago department, gives much credit to Mayor Daley. "He is the greatest public administrator I have ever known," says Wilson. "When I took this job he gave me just one instruction: 'Make the Chicago Police Department the best in the country.' He has given continuous moral and administrative support, he has seen to it that we got the funds, and when necessary, he has seen to it that we got the legislation. Without this, we never could have achieved what has been achieved." Wherever the balance of credit may lie, there is little doubt that Daley and Wilson together have written a chapter in the history of police reform that will be studied for a long time.

The reform was not all smooth sailing. As with other full-scale police modernizations, the Chicago program bucked strong headwinds, and efforts to topple Wilson were made. Discontent among certain members of the force erupted into a storm in 1961, as described in chapter three. But Wilson stood firm, Mayor Daley backed him, and civic leaders, the newspapers, and the people of Chicago rallied to him overwhelmingly. Although they didn't speak out—policemen do not openly undercut their fellow officers—a substantial portion of men on the force were in Wilson's corner. With this combination of support, Wilson had what he needed to win. "He was never in danger," a top Chicago political official told me.

And, of course, another person deserves to be remembered in the history of the Chicago reform. Richard Morrison started the whole thing when he finally found someone in the law-enforcement network who would listen to his story. A reader of Chicago's *American* wrote a letter to the paper in 1962, suggesting that Morrison should receive the Chicago Man of the Year award for having made the greatest contribution to the civic betterment of the city!

CHAPTER ELEVEN

Chicago —
Dealing with Police Abuses

Chicago Superintendent Wilson has some definite ideas about what caused corruption in the Chicago Police Department, and what causes it in other police forces. Leaning forward at his desk in his office on the fourth floor of police headquarters, he said precisely and carefully, "This force was corrupted by the citizens of Chicago."

With his steel-gray hair, high cheek bones, lean, athletic physique, ruddy face, expressive hands, and quick smile, Wilson is an engaging man who looks his role as the resourceful commander of a semimilitary organization. On the day of our interview he was wearing a blue suit and a green tie, and he is known for wearing natty tweeds.

He took a cigarette from a pack on his desk, placed it in a white holder, and lit it with a gold lighter. "The history of the problem goes a long way back into the history of the relationship of Americans and their servants," he said, snapping the lighter shut. "At Christmastime, and at other occasions as well, it has been customary to give doormen, chauffeurs, maids, cooks, and deliverymen little gifts and gratuities. There is also the matter of tipping. The whole concept of small rewards for better service permeates our civilization. It is felt that the level of service, and the special individual attention that one will get for his own problems and needs, depends on these gratuities.

"Now, there was little difficulty in transferring the concept from servants to *public* servants. It was natural to include policemen on the list of those who had rendered special help, or from whom one wanted special help. It was not necessarily prompted by an evil impulse. You gave gratuities to policemen who had rendered good and faithful service. This included police officers who guarded your place of business or your home.

"Unfortunately, it was easy to extend this to the offering of gratuities to policemen who would perform little favors that were not legal. A common example is the parking of a car in an illegal place. Both businessmen and ordinary citizens are often inconvenienced by the parking problems of a metropolis. They are glad to slip a few dollars to a policeman who is willing to overlook occasional or regular parking of a vehicle in an illegal spot."

Superintendent Wilson put down his cigarette and leaned forward, his two hands resting vertically on the desk parallel to each other, like a pair of parentheses enclosing the next area of the problem. "Now," he said, "a certain progression of events follows. Some of the more grasping policemen would, shall we say, make themselves readily available for gratuities. Businessmen and others came to understand that the policemen now *expected* the gratuities as a matter of course, and they gave the gratuities accordingly. During the holiday season, the giving of such gifts became a regular procedure. One trucking firm made it quietly known that it would pay five dollars to any cop who cared to walk in the front door of their establishment and out the back door at Christmastime. As each cop picked up his five bucks his name and star number were recorded to prevent chiselers from going through twice! The company did this as a simple business procedure. They felt—undoubtedly correctly—that the police would be more lenient with their drivers. There would either be no arrests for traffic violations, or, if an arrest took place, the firm could call friendly members of the force and seek considerate treatment."

Wilson picked up his cigarette. "Of course," he continued, "few of those who gave the gratuities stopped to reflect that they were really 'buying' special services from the police, beyond what the ordinary taxpayer would get. Similarly, few drivers stopped to think of the consequences of clipping five-dollar bills to their drivers' licenses. Note that the police didn't invent this idea. The drivers invented it. And here again, the practice was easy to rationalize. Chicago citizens said to themselves, 'Sure, I was guilty. I have paid my penalty. Instead of giving it to the city, I have given it to a nice, underpaid police officer who is helping to protect us all. As for me, it has saved me the extreme inconvenience of a day in court."

Commissioner Wilson smiled as he pursued the inexorable logic of the problem. He lays problems out piece by piece, in a tight chain of analytical detail.

"Now, things take another turn. Citizens who were careless enough to 'forget' the five-dollar bill would find traffic policemen reminding them that it would be cheaper and easier this way. Also, policemen began to stop cars for dubious or frivolous reasons, expecting the five-spot to be handed to them with the license.

"The practice of accepting payoffs from businessmen and drivers was extended to more serious crimes. If a policeman caught a burglar with a big haul, he would take part or all of the haul and let the burglar go. 'If I arrest this man,' the policeman would rationalize, 'he will be released on bond. The money will go to a bondsman and a lawyer to fix up the case.' The officer reasoned that he might just as well have that money himself.

"Now we come to the final act of the grim business, as it was played out in Summerdale. Suppose you caught a thief with no money. You could bargain with him. You could get him to perform future burglaries with you or for you, and offer him protection in exchange for a share of the haul."

With the chain of events explained, Superintendent Wilson leaned back. "When I took office," he said, "one of my first steps was to make a public announcement in which I made all this just as clear as I could. I told people that the same kind of special consideration that they were buying for small amounts, could, by the same logic, be purchased by criminals and crime syndicates for larger amounts. I believe that many people were somewhat aghast when they stopped to realize the relationship of their own conduct to police corruption and the spread of crime. When people realized that they were part of the pattern of corrupting Chicago police, they cut it out."

In addition to his public appeal, Wilson and a group of consultants created a system for checking into complaints against police that is probably the best procedure of its kind ever developed. Prior to Wilson, complaints against Chicago police officers were handled in an almost completely haphazard fashion. They went to no central source. If, as in the case of Richard Morrison, the tale was told to an individual policeman or detective, he or his immediate superior would often decide on the spot whether the allegations would be looked into or not. If a complaint was received at police headquarters or one of the district headquarters, it was simply sent "somewhere"—usually to the commander of the man's unit, who did little or nothing about it. If an officer became the subject of a series of complaints, his commander might simply call him in and say, "Listen, for gosh sakes, straighten up, will you?" "It was simply accepted prior to 1960 that the department was corrupt," says Herman Goldstein, Wilson's executive assistant.

The old system was equally capricious in cases which were investigated. "The way it used to be," says Deputy Superintendent Joseph F. Morris, head of the bureau of inspectional services and supervisor of four divisions including the internal investigation division, "a serious complaint against a policeman usually meant he was suspended pending investigation. If he was cleared he had a fight to get his back pay, and often was reinstated in an inferior job."

A typical instance occurred on November 9, 1959, when four Chicago policemen were suspended on charges made by a dope peddler that the cops had accepted bribes from him. The accusations had originally been made in August, and nothing whatever had been done about them until November, when the men were suddenly suspended. The men vigorously denied the accusations. With considerable reluctance and with obvious doubts as to the merit of the accusations, the State attorney brought the case before a grand jury, which promptly threw it out without even a vote because of its flimsiness. In the past, the peddler, when in trouble, had made similar accusations against other policemen, all of which turned out to be false. In January the four policemen were tried by the civil service board, which found them not guilty. Their accuser never even showed up. They were restored to duty as of

January 8, but without their back pay from November 10, and poorer by about $300 each that they had spent for lawyers' fees. In addition, the four men, who had all been detectives, were restored to duty as patrolmen. As to that, they had no recourse whatever. As to their back pay, to get it they would either have to file a court action, or else have a special bill introduced in the city council by a friendly alderman—one instance among thousands of the extent to which policemen were beholden to politicians for their fortunes on the force.

"The problem," says Herman Goldstein, "was to set up a system that would exercise complete control of complaints so that none could be swept under the rug, and all would be dealt with fairly." The result of this thinking was the creation of the internal investigation division. Its activities are prescribed by Police Department General Order 16, a document consisting of nine closely printed pages. The procedures outlined in General Order 16 are probably the most sophisticated ever devised to handle complaints against police and to check police corruption.

The division consists of a director, four lieutenants, twenty-five sergeants, sixty patrolmen, and three civilians, whose exclusive assignment is the handling of complaints against the police. The system—and Superintendent Wilson stresses this heavily—is designed equally to find the guilty and to protect the innocent.

The division's basic assignments are:

(1) Maintain complete records of all complaints against Chicago policemen, and their outcome;

(2) Investigate, or assign for investigation, all such complaints;

(3) Review the reports of all such investigations;

(4) When necessary, prepare cases for the department disciplinary board and the police board.

The division has four sections. The complaint section, nerve center of the operation, receives, records, assigns for investigation, reviews all cases, and maintains the records. The general investigation section handles most of the investigating work. The special investigation section handles serious accusations that, if established, would result in the initiation of criminal charges against the policeman involved. The department advocate section prepares cases, after investigation is completed, for presentation to the disciplinary board. After the disciplinary board has completed its hearings and made its recommendations, the department advocate section prepares a synopsis of the investigation and the hearing, along with the disciplinary board's recommendation, which it forwards to the superintendent of police for approval and action. The department advocate section also prepares serious cases, in which formal charges against a policeman are brought by the superintendent, for direct presentation to the police board. (This five-man blue-ribbon civilian board, created as part of the Wilson reform, supervises the entire police department and chooses the superintendent.)

When anyone calls the Chicago Police Department to complain about any phase of the work, activities, or conduct of a policeman, the call is immediately switched to the complaint desk of the internal investigation division. Anonymous calls are accepted. Persons may also come to police headquarters in person to make complaints; they are also sent directly to the internal investigation division's complaint desk.

When a supervising police officer hears any hint or rumor of misconduct by any of his men, he is required to report the information to the investigation division within one hour after he receives it, regardless of whether he believes the accusations to be true or not.

The division's full facilities are also available to innocent accused men. Any member of the police department who feels threatened by a false accusation or a contrived situation may request an investigation. If he thinks it desirable or necessary, a policeman can request such an investigation directly from the director of the division without reporting to his superiors.

At the complaint desk, the sergeant on duty takes down rough information on a work sheet at the time of receipt of a complaint. The work sheet is made in one copy only, is intended for office use, and becomes a part of the confidential file on the case. The work sheet calls for detailed information on the date, time, and place of the alleged transgression, names of witnesses, information identifying the accused police officer if the complainant does not know his name, the name and address of the complainant if he is willing to supply it, and the exact time of receipt of the complaint.

The next step is important. Information from the work sheet is transferred to a complaint register book, a bound volume containing 250 pages which have two complaint register forms to a page. Each form in the register is numbered consecutively, and numbers carry over from one register to the next. Once the case is in the register, it is thereafter identified *by its register number only*—not by the police officer's name. The register has no index so that no case can be located by the accused person's name. It is a confidential volume that can be seen only by the superintendent of police, several top officers of the department, the director of the internal investigation division, and the men assigned to keep the volume. Except in cases where the accusations are sustained, the case remains an anonymous number in the register and in the files of the division, and never enters the personnel record of the accused policeman. Innocent men are thus fully protected.

After the case is entered in the complaint register a file folder for it is set up bearing the complaint register number. A letter of information on the case is prepared, along with index cards for statistical purposes and a progress sheet on which a record of the progress of the investigation is maintained.

Complaints of a less serious nature are usually passed on to the policeman's superiors, who assign someone in their unit to conduct the investigation and report to them. Reports of such investigations must be detailed and complete, and the superior officer who assigned the investigator to the case is held responsible for the thoroughness of the report that is transmitted back to the internal investigation division.

Unless special circumstances make it undesirable, all statements made by the accuser are made known to the accused. His own full statement is made part of the record. When possible, the accuser's statement is read to the officer in the presence of the complainant so that the officer can face his accuser. Statements from witnesses are obtained and a full inquiry is made into the circumstances under which the action took place. If it is found at any time during the investigation that the complaint is clearly unfounded, the investigation is terminated and all materials are forwarded to the internal investigation division.

When his work is done the investigator classifies the complaint as follows:

(1) *Unfounded*—Allegation is false or not factual.

(2) *Exonerated*—Incident complained of occurred but was lawful and proper.

(3) *Not Sustained*—Insufficient evidence either to prove or disprove the allegation.

(4) *Sustained*—The allegation is supported by sufficient evidence.

If the complaint is classified as unfounded, exonerated, or not sustained, the policeman is so notified and is told that no record of the complaint will appear in his personnel file. In such cases the only existing record is that maintained in the complaint register book and numbered file, identifying the case by number only. As we shall see, on certain rare occasions this information is immensely valuable in protecting a policeman against later false charges.

In sustained cases, disciplinary action may take the form of an oral reprimand, a written reprimand, extra duty, suspension, or dismissal from the force. Extra duty is the most widely used form of discipline—"it is always possible to utilize additional manpower," Thomas J. Ryan, director of the division, observes. Extra duty is a form of punishment in lieu of suspension without pay. This penalizes the officer through loss of cherished time off, but not through his pay check.

In cases involving suspension up to a period of twenty-nine days, or in cases in which the officer states his preference for suspension instead of extra duty, he has the right to a hearing before the disciplinary board. All members of the police department holding the rank of captain or above are members of the board; a panel, composed of one officer of exempt rank as presiding officer and two captains, hears each individual case. The hearing is arranged by the department advocate, who forwards all records of the case to the board panel. The panel studies all documents, hears any accused man who wishes to appear, and sometimes orders the accused to appear. Its findings are forwarded to the superintendent of police for final action.

In serious cases in which the department is seeking suspension of more than thirty days or dismissal from the force, the case is heard by the police board itself. The superintendent presents the evidence in support of the complaint and the respondent may offer evidence in defense. He may be represented by counsel and every opportunity is given him to rebut the accusations.

After each case has been completed and the punishment specified, the file is checked by an internal investigation division review officer for discrepancies, omissions, irregularities, or missing documents. When the investigation has been made within the man's unit, the quality of the investigative work is studied. The quality of the investigative work is usually high, but weak links must be watched. "A few supervisors have a tendency to take a paternal attitude toward their men," says Ryan. "They see no evil and hear no evil as far as their 'boys' are concerned. They turn their back on a bad situation hoping that it will go away. Here lies the seed bed of potential scandals."

The division has cracked down hard on bribery. In December 1960 Theodore Samuels, a Federal Aviation Agency employee, was stopped by policeman Francis Elliott for running through a red light. Elliott told Samuels that he would "excuse him for ten dollars." Samuels told Elliott that he had only traveler's checks with him but was willing to pay the policeman if he could go back to his hotel for some money. Samuels returned to the hotel while Elliott waited outside. But Samuels, who like most other Chicagoans, now knew of the internal investigation division's drive against bribery, put in a call to the division and told them the story. In less than a minute other policemen arrived at the rear entrance of the hotel, and gave Samuels a marked ten-dollar bill. Samuels went out front and handed the bill to Elliott. As soon as Elliott accepted it he was seized and arrested. He was suspended from the force, tried, and found guilty.

Meanwhile, in accordance with Wilson's order, police began to arrest would-be bribers. Patrolman James Sinclair made such an arrest of a motorist. Asked if many motorists offer him bribes, he replied, "Not in so many words. This fellow actually put the money in my hand. They'll say things like, 'Isn't there some way we can arrange this?' or, 'Isn't there something I can do for you?' "

It took only a few cases like these, and traffic bribery dropped to the vanishing point. Even among those inclined to accept bribes, a policeman could never know whether the solicitation of the bribe would result in his arrest. Citizens tempted to offer bribes were deterred by the same fear. In one area, however, the investigation division's statistics showed a problem. A small number of police still on the take had apparently decided that out-of-state motorists were the safe bet for shaking down, since they would be unlikely to know of the division and even less likely to bother making a complaint after they returned to their homes from their visits to Chcago.

In July 1963, at 3 A.M., a truck from California ran through a stop sign in a warehouse district in Chicago. The driver thought the street was deserted, but a policeman materialized out of the shadows and flagged the truck down.

Interstate truck drivers don't like to get tickets. It annoys their employers and makes a black mark on the drivers' records. Policemen know this. The policemen looked at the driver's license and then said, "Why don't we hold court here?" The driver reached into his pocket and silently handed the cop a ten-spot. The cop nodded, handed back the driver's license, and walked away.

The truck driver's driving partner was amused. But the driver didn't think it was funny. All the way back to the West Coast he mulled it over, and when he returned to Los Angeles he put in a call to the Chicago Police Department. "I want to complain about a cop taking a bribe," he said. "I gave him the bribe and now I'm sorry." The call was switched to the internal investigation division. The driver, who wondered if anyone would really be interested in his tale, found that the division was very interested indeed. The complaint desk took full particulars on the case.

"When will you be in town again?" the sergeant on the phone asked him.

"We're coming in again next week," the driver replied.

"When will you be arriving?"

"About 2:30 in the morning."

"We'll meet you and get full details," the sergeant said.

When Director Ryan learned of the case, he realized that it might turn out to be the big break in the out-of-state bribery situation. He told Superintendent Wilson about it, and Wilson agreed. "Get to the bottom of it," he said.

The next week, when the driver arrived in Chicago, he kept an appointment with investigators at a prearranged location. The investigators took a statement from him. On a subsequent trip the internal investigation division arranged a line-up of policemen from whom the driver was asked to pick the man he had bribed. Without hesitation the driver pointed to one of the men in the line-up, saying, "That's him."

The case really began to warm up. For one thing, by coincidence, the police officer picked out of the line-up had formerly been a truck driver himself, and both were members of the same union. Subtle fraternal pressures were now brought on the driver to drop the whole thing. The driver stubbornly refused. He then began to receive anonymous phone calls, threatening violence against him when he came to Chicago. To protect him, the internal investigation division assigned men to meet him at the city line during each of his trips to Chicago and to escort him at all times while he was in the city.

In November 1963 the trial was held. The truck driver was an absolutely convincing witness, and the policeman was convicted. Complaints of shaking down of out-of-state drivers swiftly ebbed. It was a big change from the days in 1959 when Richard Morrison couldn't interest the Chicago Police Department in his story. A few men on the force were probably not too happy with the new way of life. "It probably cut the incomes of a few cops in half," says one high official of the department. But most policemen reacted to the new system with relief. One admitted privately that in former years he had taken a few bribes— "but only when they offered it—I never asked. It was the system. Everybody was doing it, or at least they talked about it, so we said, 'What the hell,' and went along. But I never felt right about it. I'm glad it's over with."

In its investigations, the division takes the time to build an airtight case when the allegations prove to be correct. One anonymous tip accused a policeman of being involved in the sale of narcotics. Careful investigation proved that the charges were true. The division filmed an actual exchange of money between the cop and a narcotics user, then arrested the policeman when he reported for duty. The policeman is now in the penitentiary.

The division is similarly thorough in anything that even smells faintly like police involvement in burglary. The Illinois Central Railroad reported to the Chicago Police Department the theft of two immense reels of copper trolley wire. An Illinois Central yard watchman recalled that, on the night of the theft, he saw a pickup truck in the yard. The driver simply said, "I'm a cop. I'm lost." The internal investigation division discovered that a pickup truck of the type described by the night watchman had, in fact, been rented by a certain Chicago policeman from a rent-a-car agency on the night of the crime. Intensive detective work revealed that the same policeman had also rented a power saw shortly before the theft. Investigators reasoned that he might have used the saw to cut up the wire into disposable lengths. On the dirt floor of the garage on the policeman's property, investigators found minute traces of copper powder on the ground which had escaped the policeman's attention when he cleaned up the garage after sawing up the wire. The policeman denied everything, but he was arrested and convicted—the division's case was tight as a drum.

Many investigations have shown the depth of mutual involvement between corrupted policemen and corrupting citizens. A trucking association complained that policemen were shaking them down on occasions when trucks were overweight. Investigators learned about weight laws from the Illinois secretary of state and began surprise weighing of trucks. They found the same thing that Illinois State Police investigators found—that overloading of trucks, instead of being unusual, was a universal practice among many trucking firms. These truckers had sought to corrupt certain Chicago policemen in order to continue this evasion and had succeeded. Two cops were arrested. At the same time, Chicago police cracked down on the truckers and, for the first time in anybody's memory, secured substantial compliance with the state's weight laws.

The internal investigation division has found that one of its big problems is to keep people interested in the complaints that they make against police long enough for the division to complete its work. People who report legitimate grievances often show little desire to see the problem really corrected. In June 1963 an executive of a carnival playing in Warsaw, Indiana, reported that one of the carnival's trucks had been stolen. It was recovered near Chicago. The executive subsequently complained to the internal investigation division that it had cost him $150 in bribes to Chicago policemen to get his truck back in a hurry. Subsequently the division had great difficulty in contacting the man. He apparently decided that his complaint against the police was unwise since it might harm his future relations with them. An internal investigation official finally went to Montgomery, Alabama, where the carnival was playing. There the executive signed a statement. The next step was to have him identify the policemen in a line-up. The man said he would be in Chicago in December; but when he arrived in town he again became impossible to contact. Director Ryan himself finally visited the man's hotel. He was told that the man was not in. Waiting for hours, Director Ryan finally caught a glimpse of him and persuaded him to finish what he had started. Every case is followed through with this type of thoroughness.

In addition to investigating complaints, the division initiates its own periodic checks in sensitive areas of potential police involvement in corruption. "Ambulance chasing" is such an area. Periodically, investigators question people involved in accidents. Did the policemen who handled the case recommend a lawyer? A repair shop? The knowledge that periodic spot checks are conducted acts as a further deterrent to policemen who might be tempted to enter into kickback arrangements.

In 1904 the Chicago Police Department hired a certain Colonel Piper, a retired Army man, to check on the performance of the men. Colonel Piper was a martinet. He checked all the small things and missed all the big ones. The Chicago chief gave him a group of sergeants as inspectors. These men became known as "Piper's Eyes," and later as "Piperisers." They ruthlessly ferreted out such instances of evil-doing as smoking cigarettes or drinking coffee during duty hours and reporting for roll call with buttons unshined. Piper held kangaroo courts and meted out severe punishments, such as docking a man three days' pay for the most minor offenses. The Piperisers were thoroughly hated, and the system generated so much bitterness that it was discontinued in a few years. It was reinstituted in 1919, and again lasted only a couple of years.

"The Piperisers were never forgiven and never forgotten," said Director Ryan. "I joined the Chicago force in December 1932. I saw the former Piperisers who were still on the force being universally shunned. Even their sons, if they joined the force, were fingered and utterly isolated.

"That is what we faced when we set up this division under the superintendent's orders in 1960. We wondered if we were going to become members of a new hated legion. At first we had trouble getting high-caliber men into the unit. They were afraid of being shunned by their fellows on the force. But we have been building up a record of fairness and today we are accepted as an indispensable part of the force. Checking on complaints against policemen isn't always pleasant, but most men now realize that it is necessary. The realization has become deeper as we have succeeded in rooting out real criminal activity, and at the same time have cleared literally thousands of indiscriminately or unjustly accused men."

The internal investigation division considers its work in protecting the unjustly accused just as important as finding the guilty. "Defending unjustly accused members of the force is a heavy responsibility," says Director Ryan. The division's experience bears out his statement. It has found that many people who see money pass between a policeman, on or off duty, and any other person, assume that bribery is taking place. Men who have given five dollars to their mothers have been turned in for bribery. It has also found that many complaints against policemen are turned in, not by the supposedly aggrieved person, but by witnesses, bystanders, and relatives, who actually turn out to know little or nothing about the situation. Under questioning, many of these people quickly acknowledge that they really do not know what happened. When the aggrieved person himself is questioned, he will often deny any knowledge of wrongdoing which others have reported.

In other instances people refuse to believe the truth because it does not accord with their preconceptions. One case involved events which occurred during a night basketball game between two high schools that were deadly rivals. Some of the visiting school's students assembled inside the gym, and a number of them began to taunt the policeman who was on duty at the event. Finally two big football players, without provocation, assaulted the cop and pummeled him. The policeman struggled with his assailants, and one of them struck his head on the side of a shower stall during the scuffle.

The boy's parents accused the policeman of attacking the two big fellows and hitting the injured boy with his night stick. The internal investigation division took state ments from many witnesses, found that the allegation was entirely false, and so informed the parents—who would not believe a word of it. "What do you mean, our boy attacked the cop?" the mother raged to Director Ryan. "We didn't raise our kids like that!" Director Ryan, who was fully satisfied with the investigation's results, stood by the accused policeman. "You're a crook!" the boy's mother finally screamed at Ryan on the telephone. She hung up and that was the last that the Chicago Police Department heard of the case.

As the division's defense of falsely accused men has become increasingly well known, it has made some friends among members of the force who were at first deeply skeptical. In one case a detective lieutenant arrested an out-of-state sex pervert. The sex pervert promptly filed counter-charges against the policeman. An investigation showed the charges to be completely unfounded. Two years later the lieutenant called the division. "I've been notified that that guy is now suing me for false arrest," said the lieutenant. "I sure hope you guys still have that file on that investigation you made." "We certainly do," Director Ryan replied. The file, of course, could not be located by name, since all cases are filed by their complaint numbers to protect identities. But the numbers run serially, and an individual's file can be found when the approximate date of the complaint is known. The file was located and forwarded to the corporation counsel's office for preparation of the lieutenant's defense. Two Chicago policemen were also sent to Michigan to gather further information to assist in the defense. When he learned of the nature and extent of the evidence against him, the pervert dropped his suit. "I'm one guy who is plenty grateful to the division," said the lieutenant.

The division receives other endorsements from policemen, often through the grapevine. When the division cracks a serious case there is often a "feedback" through various anonymous sources in the department that have long suspected the situation. The general tenor of this feedback is "You got the right guy that time. He's been long overdue."

As an integral part of its work, the division has been compiling, studying, and breaking down statistics on complaints against policemen. These statistics are the most extensive of their kind in existence, and they throw a fascinating light on problems of police corruption and police misconduct. The most impressive figure of all is that, of the thousands of complaints registered against Chicago policemen, well over half turn out to be completely groundless, and only 15 percent are sustained.

In 1963 the division completed action on 4,178 complaints against policemen. Of these, 2,659 were classified as unfounded, and another 270 as exonerated. Another 678 were classified as not sustained. Only 571 were sustained.

The division has also found that nearly half the complaints registered against policemen are for indebtedness. The complainants say that the accused policeman owes money which he has not paid in a reasonable length of time. Most of these complaints are settled by conducting direct discussions with the complainant and the accused policeman, and working out a payment schedule. Such cases, when settled in this fashion, are not entered in the complaint register book. A total of 3,879 indebtedness complaints were made against Chicago policemen in 1963, of which only 435 proved sufficiently intractable to enter in the complaint register book. The total of 4,178 registered complaints against Chicago policemen for 1963, therefore, includes only 435 of the nearly 4,000 indebtedness complaints. No one knows if a similar proportion of indebtedness complaints would be registered against an average sampling of the American community if it were subjected to the same kind of disciplinary and reporting procedures as the Chicago police.

Bribery complaints totaled 309 in 1963. Of these, 167 were traffic cases, of which only 13 were sustained. The remaining 142 were in other categories, of which 14 were sustained. These figures appear to reflect two important things—the effectiveness of the anticorruption program in the department, and the alacrity with which people accuse policemen of crimes when there is little or no substance to the charge.

Other features of the Chicago statistics are interesting. During 1963, 292 complaints were registered against Chicago policemen by other policemen who were willing to identify themselves. In addition, 416 anonymous complaints were received, many of which, the division believes, came from policemen who did not wish to identify themselves. The number of policemen complainants has been increasing as honest policemen have gained increasing confidence in the new system.

Other patterns reveal themselves. Most policemen who get in trouble are young men, new to the force. Another prominent group consists of men who have been on the force five to ten years, who have accumulated a good record and some commendations, then suddenly start slipping. The division has been analyzing the kinds of men involved in both patterns, and the results of the analysis will be used in refining selection procedures. Careful analysis is also made of every case in which men are dismissed from the force. Something was obviously wrong in such a person's selection. The police department is trying to profit from the lessons learned.

Individual instances of corruption have not been completely eliminated from the Chicago force. They probably never can be, from this or any other police force. But there is little doubt that Superintendent Wilson has put a drastic end to widespread "free-enterprising" by Chicago police—something that most people were quite convinced could never be accomplished. As early as Christmas, 1960, the first year of Wilson's administration, a businessman who owns a small factory on Chicago's West Side told reporters that for the first time in his memory not one policeman had come into his place of business looking for a donation. "We used to have a regular procession of them," he said.

Superintendent Wilson is an outspoken opponent of civilian review boards that investigate complaints against police. "Discipline," he says, emphasizing every word, "is a function of command. It should not be divorced from operational responsibility. The answer to the problem of police misconduct and corruption is not the creation of an outside disciplinary agency. The answer is the creation of the right kind of a system within the force, consisting of men who know and understand police work, to protect the innocent and punish the guilty." Scholars and municipal government experts do not all agree with Superintendent Wilson on this problem. But none can deny that Chicago's internal investigation division is the most impressive possible argument for his side of the case.

CHAPTER TWELVE

Two Cops
Who Became Thieves

I talked with many psychologists, sociologists, and criminologists about the question of why a policeman becomes
a criminal. I also talked it over with certain especially
qualified experts—cops who had been involved in crime
and had been caught.

I explained my project over the phone to the warden of
the state penitentiary where ex-policemen John Blake
and Robert Hastings * were serving their time.

"Come on down," the warden said. "We'll have them
ready in the conference room and you can talk with them
as long as you like."

I arrived early the next morning. After my identity and
my mission had been confirmed, a series of three elec-
trically operated iron-barred gates slid silently open. In
the receiving room I was quickly and expertly "shaken
down" by a guard and the contents of my briefcase were
minutely scrutinized. I talked briefly with the warden, a
man with a lot of calm assurance and an infectious twinkle
in his eye, and was then led to the conference room where

* The names, and a few minor details of their stories, have been changed.
Everything else is recorded here as they said it.

the men were waiting for me. The prison guard left and the three of us were alone.

Blake and Hastings stood up tall and straight and shook hands with me without smiling. They were wearing faded blue dungarees with their state prison numbers stenciled on both shirt and pants. I had no trouble envisioning them wearing the uniform and badge of policemen. I found myself trying to envision them in dark stores and warehouses at night, pulling the burglaries that had brought them here. That was harder.

I explained to them that I wasn't interested in the details of their cases—I could read the papers as well as the next fellow. I was interested in knowing the atmosphere of the police department and the community. Among other things, I said, I wondered if such things could go on without others in the police department knowing about it. Both men smiled.

"There's no doubt in my mind that lots of people knew," said Blake, and Hastings nodded his assent.

"Did the public know?" I asked.

"The public doesn't care," said Blake. "They tend to despise police and to assume that cops have got their hands in the till. People are glad to see us if their daughters are being raped, but generally their interest in the police, and their opinion of us, is pretty low."

"There are other problems," said Hastings. "You can usually assume that you make at least one enemy every time you handle a case properly. Nobody likes a cop to stop them for speeding, much less some of the other things you catch leading citizens doing. After five or six years on the force you have made a lot of enemies in the community. I think this contributes to public dislike of the police. A policeman gets little support for doing his job well. To be a good cop you have to know that you will be backed when you do the right thing. You usually get no such backing from the community. What they say in the Rotary Clubs and what happens out in the squad car or out on the beat at night are two different things. And you not only have little community backing for doing your job, but all too often you can't count on having the backing of the higher echelons of the department itself."

"Do you feel that any of this contributed to the situation in which the police scandal took place?"

"Well, there's such a thing as getting too fancy about it." Blake smiled. "No one stuck a gun in my back and told me that I had to steal."

His comment reminded me of what the warden had said to me just before I entered the conference room: "They have gotten along all right in the prison population. They aren't going around blaming the world. They have regrets but no excuses."

"When did you join the force?" I asked Blake.

"In 1951. After high school I did construction work and then took out a general contractor's license. I was doing all right but I had always wanted to be a policeman. I took a big cut in income when I joined the force.

"When did you first get an inkling that things weren't all on the up-and-up?"

"It didn't take long. We had four weeks of training, and then went on the job as probationary patrolmen. I was a pretty eager cop, and right away I caught two burglars stealing a generator from a warehouse. It turned out that they were both policemen. What could I do? I was a rookie on probation and it would have been my word against theirs. On the force, if you don't shut up and go along you don't last out your probation. One or two bad reports on you filed by veteran cops and you're dropped without even being told why."

"What about you?" I asked Hastings.

"I liked the idea of being a cop too," he said. "I quit high school in the tenth grade and went to work as a guard in the city jail. Then I spent three years in the Army as an MP. I liked it. When I got out of the service I went to work in the county sheriff's office. I thought a lot of the sheriff and he liked me. One day he came to me and said, 'John, they're giving exams for openings on the city police force. Why don't you go down there and take them? I think you'd make a good cop.' So I took the exams, passed them, and joined the force. That was in 1953."

"What was your pay?"

"It was just under $300 a month. My wife and I had one child then. We had talked it over and had decided that we could squeak through somehow until I became a first-class patrolman and got a little more pay. I have to admit that it would have been hard for me to choose something that paid less."

"When did you first get wind of odd goings-on?"

"Well, I went through the four-week training period, which wasn't much of anything. Then I was assigned as a probationary patrolman, and rode in a patrol car with a senior officer from whom I was supposed to learn the ropes.

"A few nights later I was driving the car, and my partner told me to pull into a parking lot. The lot was dark, the attendants had gone home, and nobody was around. My partner got out, walked down the line of parked cars, and smashed in the wing window of one of them with his night stick. He reached in, unlocked the door, and removed from the seat a portable sewing machine and a Norelco electric razor. He took the sewing machine and put it in the trunk of the police car. 'My old lady's been wanting one of these.' he explained. Then he tossed the Norelco razor to me. He must have seen the expression on my face because he said, 'If you tell, I'll say you did it. Who are they going to believe—a rookie like you, or me? Take the razor, kid, and don't be worried.'

"I couldn't sleep when I got off duty that night. I didn't know what to do or what to think. For one thing, there's a strong feeling that policemen have, that you are loyal to your fellow cops. For another thing, I knew that he was right—if I squealed on him the only person who would get hurt would be me. A rookie can't change the way things are. Even if they were to take my word against his—which was darned unlikely—I would be a marked man.

"The next day I took that Norelco razor and I threw it in the river. Then I went to see my old boss the sheriff, whom I respected so much. 'Sheriff,' I said, 'I don't want to rat on anybody and I ask you please not to force me to rat. All I want to say is, there are things going on that I don't like and I don't want any part of. I don't want anything to do with stealing and things like that. What I want to know is, can I please have my old job back here in the sheriff's office, working for you?'

"His reply bowled me over. 'I know what you mean, son,' he said. 'I know what's going on. Everyone knows what's going on. Stick it out. You don't have to participate in it if you don't want to. After you've put in a year, you can ask for a transfer to the traffic division if you want, or you can drive your own patrol car.'

"I spent quite a few days trying to absorb these revelations that were coming to me. I was terribly disoriented and upset. You may think I was naïve, but the truth is, when I joined the force I had no idea that this was the way things were run."

"When did the next revelation come?" I asked.

"Well," he said, "I began to learn more about how things worked. You couldn't always expect to be backed up. When I had been on the force a little while a kid patrolman came to me very upset. He had issued a ticket for speeding to the editor of one of the local papers. This editor swings a lot of weight and the police brass don't want to be on the bad side of him. He had been roaring along the highway to the airport to catch a plane and the kid patrolman had flagged him down. The guy was purple in the face and said, "I'm the editor of the Daily Blat and I've got to catch a plane.' The kid said, 'I don't care if you're the Queen of Sheba, you were doing eighty miles an hour and you ain't going to drive like that on this road,' and he wrote out a ticket. 'You'll regret it,' the editor said. The next day the kid was called in and told that he was being reassigned. He was taken out of the car and was put on a night beat in one of the roughest parts of town. The kid loved to drive the car and loved being a highway cop, but there was nothing anybody could do about it." (The newspaper of which this man is editor, incidentally, conducted a lofty campaign to "weed out police corruption" when Blake and Hastings were apprehended stealing.)

"Did you have any political problems?" I asked Blake.

"I got into trouble on a job I was doing on the East Side," Blake said. "It was a rough area and there were lots of muggings, rollings, and break-ins. One day the lieutenant called in me and another fellow and said, 'We're assigning you two to night duty in this area. It's a rough situation, and I want you to get in there and break it up.' The other fellow and I liked the assignment, and we decided that we *would* break it up. When cops make a decision like that you'd be surprised what they can do.

"After a few nights on the beat we noticed that certain groups of guys were hanging around together at various places, apparently doing nothing, just hanging around. The men on the day shift told us that these same guys would hang around during the day, too, doing nothing. My partner and I put in a lot of extra time on the problem, talking together and planning. We found out who most of those guys were and where they lived. We began to watch their movements very closely. Within two months we had caught more than half of them in the act, rolling, mugging, and breaking in. The rest of the gang started to break up and drift away—the word was out that the new cops meant business. The crime rate in that little area we were working started to drop. We were cited for our work, and the councilman for the area was tickled to death. He came to our CO, and he said, 'That guy Blake has done a great job in my district. I want him promoted to detective as of the first of the month.' My CO called me in and told me I was being promoted.

"But a few nights later on my beat I saw a commotion in a gutter outside a bar. The councilman's sister-in-law owns the bar, and every once in a while she would get drunk and would go on a tear. Well, there she was, drunk, beating some drunk fellow who was lying in the gutter, with the spike of her high-heeled shoe, and really hurting him plenty. I arrested her and charged her with creating a disturbance. In the station house she screamed at me that her brother-in-law had the right connections in town and she would see to it that I paid for what I had done. When she went before the municipal judge he immediately dismissed the charges against her. The next day my CO called me in and said that due to circumstances beyond his control my appointment to the detective bureau had been cancelled. I was never considered for the detective bureau again."

"Did you ever walk a beat?" I asked Hastings.

"No," said Hastings, "I continued in the car, and I began to see more and more. One thing is, the very nature of a policeman's work brings him up against terrific temptations. I got a really clear picture of this one night soon after the parking-lot incident. A cop is like everybody else, probably—he can drive around on the job and his mind can be on the overdue bill that his wife came to him with and that he doesn't know how he is going to pay. That was the way it was with me on this night.

"My partner and I noticed that the door of a small uptown shop was open. We radioed the dispatcher that we were entering. That's standard procedure. If you are going to enter a premises in the line of duty you call the dispatcher to tell him. He usually sends out a covering car with a sergeant or lieutenant in it, to give you help or protection if you need it. Well, we radioed the dispatcher, then we pulled up the car and went in with our guns drawn. A thing like that is a real kind of a case—you never know if some shots are going to start coming at you from some dark corner. But nobody was there.

"We put up our guns and my partner walked to the safe and started fiddling carefully with the dial. The door popped right open. 'I thought so,' he said. 'They left it on daylock. When they do that, all you have to do is turn it to one right number and she opens.' He reached inside and pulled out a wad of money. Then he looked at me with complete earnestness. 'You know, Bob,' he said. 'They don't lose a thing. They will claim it on their insurance—in fact, they'll claim more than they lost, and they'll get it without question. Now don't tell me that you can't use a little of this.' We ended up splitting it, and we gave some to the sergeant who came down to cover the case. He needed some too. It was the first money I took. I wasn't 'hooked' yet—that is, I wasn't a regular thief or burglar. But I had taken my first stolen money.

"Soon after that my partner and I surprised a couple of guys hauling some merchandise out of a warehouse. We caught them in a dark alley, drew our guns, and told them to get their hands up. They quickly identified themselves—they were policemen. My partner and I put up our guns. I suddenly realized that I probably didn't care very much any more. I was closer to being hooked."

He stopped for a moment, and took out a cigarette. It remained unlit in his hands as he went on.

"It's funny," he said, "but I think the thing that hooked me was the thing that happened a few nights later. It was a small thing, nothing compared to kinds of jobs we were in after that. But you know, we were talking about the revelations I had. This was my next revelation, and it brought me in contact with the business community of the town.

"One night my partner and I were cruising down a dark alley late at night. A light snow was falling, and it had been falling since about 8 P.M. There were no tire tracks or footprints in the alley. Suddenly I noticed that the back door of a warehouse seemed to be open about a foot. There was a timber jammed up against it. It looked as if the door had drifted open a short way until it had been stopped by the timber.

" 'Stop the car,' I said to my partner. He stopped the car, we put the spotlight on the door, and I walked over. There was no sign that the door had been forced. Still, I liked to do things thoroughly. 'Call the dispatcher and tell him I'm entering,' I said. Then I went in and turned on the light.

"It was a small warehouse belonging to a manufacturer of fur coats. There were coats on racks and piles of skins around. Things were in order and I saw no sign of burglary.

"In a few minutes the lieutenant pulled up in a second car, and he had the owner of the place with him. The owner came in and walked halfway down the center aisle. Suddenly he gasped.

" 'My God!' he said. 'They're gone!'

" 'What's gone?' I asked.

" 'Over against the wall there,' he said excitedly. 'I had piles of skins on pallets. They're gone!'

" 'Pallets and all?'

"He didn't bat an eyelash. 'Pallets and all!' he said.

" 'How many skins were there?'

" 'A couple of hundred of them.'

" 'What were they worth?'

" 'Between six dollars and seven and a half each.'

"This meant a loss of twelve to fifteen hundred dollars. I was skeptical. 'Look,' I said. 'I don't think anybody took anything here. There's no sign that the door was forced. It's been snowing since about 8 P.M. and there were no footprints or car tracks of any kind anywhere in the alley before my partner and I pulled in here.'

"He turned on me furiously. 'Are you doubting my word?' he shouted. Then he looked at me and his tone changed. 'By the way,' he said with a smile, 'do you fellows know your wives' sizes? We're grateful to you for the protection you give us. I'd like to give you each a coat for what you've done here.'

"I don't know if you can understand it. But somehow that was the end. 'Yes,' I said, 'I know my wife's size and I'll take one.'

" 'What about your patrol partner?' the man asked.

" 'He'll take one too,' I said.

" 'And how about the lieutenant outside?'

" 'I *know* he'll take one,' I said—and I was right.

"After we had all gotten our coats the lieutenant said to me, 'Fill out a loss report.' I filled it out, describing the loss just the way the man told me, and the man signed it.

"The next day the loss report went through the detective bureau and a detective called me in. 'Do you think that stuff was really stolen?' he asked me. 'I don't know,' I told him. 'All I know is, if you want a nice new fur coat for your wife you can go over there and get one.' The detective promptly went over and got himself a coat. The loss report went in to the insurance company and the insurance company paid off with no muss or fuss."

I turned to Blake. "Did you run into things like that?"

He nodded. "After we got going regularly on our burglaries," he said, "businessmen would come to us and would make it clear that they wouldn't mind if somebody came along and broke into their places. They would even tell us how much money a thief could expect to find if he broke in on a given night. When we would crack the places, sure enough, there would be just the amount of money they said. It was sort of our pay. The owners of the places would then file insurance claims for amounts larger than they had lost, and the claims would always be paid.

"We used to be able to compare what we actually got with the claims that the owners made. I remember one case where a policeman broke into a bar. He had no deal with the owner in this case—he just broke in. He couldn't find a nickel, so he helped himself to about a dozen bottles of first-class booze. The owner filed a report on the burglary saying that he had lost $1,400 in cash."

"Did you continue to do good police work when you weren't involved in jobs?" I asked.

"Well, yes and no," Blake replied. "You can put a cop in a car or on a beat, but you can't make him work. How much he sees is up to him. You can be on the job for eight hours, and you can see everything, or you can see nothing. It may seem odd to you, but all the while Hastings and I were in these things, we were also cops, and we liked it, and we wanted to be good ones. We soon learned not to get mixed up in certain kinds of trouble, and not to report certain things. Our progress on the force and our security and our pensions depended more on what we didn't do in those areas than on what we did do. But where we could, we did good work. A fellow who had pulled a number of burglaries while he was a cop on the force, shot it out one night with some real burglars. He had walked into one of those open-door things, like Hastings was telling you about, and there were three burglars in there who had the drop on him and started shooting. He shot back, killed one, and captured the other two, while catching a slug in his arm. He risked his life to protect that place from a burglary, when it might just as well have been him who was doing the job!"

"During one year I had a cruising partner in my car who wasn't a burglar," said Hastings. "It was great and we did good work. In that year I made fourteen major felony arrests, and one of them cracked a big national pornography ring. It felt good to wear a badge in that year."

"Does the pay problem have a lot to do with police corruption?"

They were surprisingly hesitant in giving their answer.

"To some extent," Blake finally said. "I think that where the pay problem makes the biggest difference is in the initial recruiting. It greatly limits the number and kind of people that will go on the force. Our force was so hard pressed to get recruits that they were taking many immature young fellows. Now if there's one thing I think a policeman needs it's maturity and common sense. Twenty-two is very young to toss a kid into the kind of thing we found ourselves in, without much experience and with a deep desire to 'make the grade' in the esteem of the older men. A kid that young wants to be accepted by the big boys on the force. If the big boys are cracking safes the kid will be a little horrified, but he'll think that the mature thing to do is to hide your little-baby reaction and be cool like the big fellows.

"Also, we got a fair number of people on the force who had turned to the police because nobody was willing to pay them a decent wage. I admit that after you joined the force your money problems would tempt you to steal, but I think a much more important factor was the kind of assortment of people we got on the force in the first place because of the low pay and the low community opinion of the work."

"Blake is right, we used to get quite a collection," said Hastings. "And the police brass paid little attention to all kinds of obvious things about these people. For instance, out of every graduating class of twenty-five new rookies, two or three would go out and buy saps. You know what they are?"

I shook my head.

"A sap is a little thing four or five inches long, covered with leather, with lead inside it. It has a thong on it and you can carry it in your hand. You can kill a man with a sap, and they are illegal. But out of every class several guys would buy them, and would carry them around quite openly on the job, and none of the higher-ups said a thing. You'd think they'd be a lot more alert to spot the kind of guy who took that kind of approach to his work, but they weren't. They couldn't afford to—recruits were too scarce.

"Then there are the gun-conscious guys. They think about their gun all the time. You can spot them a mile off. There are some of them on the force, and these are the kinds of guys who are looking for a chance to shoot, and who are going to shoot somebody sooner or later in a situation where it isn't necessary. Nothing is done about these guys; nobody pays any attention, and they stay on the force along with everybody else."

"Would you go back on the force again if everything could be wiped clean?" I asked.

You couldn't help noticing the flicker of light in their eyes, but they shook their heads no.

"I loved being a cop," said Blake, "and I'll always feel that way. Once you have worn that badge you're a cop at heart all your life, no matter what you do or no matter where you end up—even here. But let me say something that will sound funny to you. I'd rather be here in this jail than be on the force. Here you get the feeling that there is justice at the top. You do your work well here and it's noticed. You stay out of trouble and you do your work and before long you have a better job, a more responsible one. They aren't giving you anything free, but they are sitting back waiting to see how you turn out. If you turn out all right and if you work hard, they come right along and meet you halfway. That's the difference—here you feel that that guy at the top is tough but fair. And you feel that nobody is going to be able to get to him behind your back and sell him a bill of goods, or persuade him not to back you if you're doing OK. It's a relief.

"Liking police work is something I'll never lose. But the real truth is, after ten years on the force, I'm afraid I had reached the point of feeling, 'Nobody else cares, and why the hell should I?' "

CHAPTER THIRTEEN

The Road to Reform

There are at least three major dimensions to the problem of police corruption. The first is that a large proportion of the nation's law-enforcement machinery is badly financed and badly out of date. The second involves inconsistent and badly thought-out laws, especially in the field of gambling. The third is the problem of civic indifference, civic neglect, and, sometimes, active or passive implication of large segments of the community in police crime and police-criminal combinations.

The seeds of scandal are sown at the very beginning of the process of creating United States police forces, through low recruiting standards and the practical necessity faced by many forces of taking almost any warm body that shows up.

Recruiting problems are grave even in a city such as Los Angeles, whose chief of police, William H. Parker, is a colorful figure with a national reputation, and whose police force enjoys unusually high public support and prestige. "Our great difficulty," says Parker, "is attracting sufficient numbers of young men to the police service who have the mental and physical qualifications to perform this rather intricate task in the field of human relations. Our policemen start at $545 a month. At the end of the third year their pay is $641 a month. This is one of the highest pay scales for policemen in the nation. But I must tell you that, though we have hired every eligible male who has offered himself to the police service of this city since the end of World War II, our net gain in officers last year [1962] was only sixty over what we had at the start of the year." The Los Angeles force has 4,700 men.

In other cities, the situation has reached a state of near-crisis. At the time of this writing the St. Louis police force is short 374 men. Houston is 747 men short. In New York it has been impossible to provide the additional police for which the public clamored in 1964 after a wave of murders, violence, and rioting.

Along with low recruiting standards often goes a low level of professional training. On a number of big-city forces today, and on a majority of small-town forces, training consists of little more than teaching the recruit how to shoot a gun and how and when to make an arrest. Many police learn little about modern methods of police work, investigation, and criminology, and even less about modern techniques of leadership, administration, and management.

After the initial, brief period of training as recruits, many policemen never receive any kind of in-service training throughout their entire careers, such as, for example, the armed forces provide for men who begin assuming broader responsibilities as they rise in rank. The initial weakness is thus carried up the chain of command as men are promoted. Lack of adequate knowledge and training at the command level means lack of control. The stage for scandal is thus fully set. "Of those scandals that have reached serious proportions," says the IACP's John Ingersoll, "almost all have one common denominator: weak leadership."

After conducting surveys of more than a score of major police departments in the United States, Ingersoll has come to believe that many forces fall into a "fifteen-fifteen-seventy pattern." Fifteen percent of many forces, he believes, consist of men who are incorruptible, regardless of the pattern of morality on the rest of the force and in the community. At the other end of the spectrum, and partially because of the present low level of recruiting and selection, about 15 percent of many forces consists of corrupt or easily corruptible personalities. The remaining 70 percent in the middle are more or less inclined to lean in the direction of the prevailing winds. If corruption gains a foothold, some of these men in the middle will be dragged along. Others, while not participating, will do nothing to expose the wrongdoers, and will often undertake small activities or "favors" to shield them. On the other hand, good leadership within the department, backed by a good moral tone in the community, brings the large group of policemen "in the middle" toward a high level of integrity and performance.

Steps are being taken to attack these extreme deficiencies in American law enforcement that have been so dramatically highlighted by the scandals. By far the most important initiative has come from within the police profession. The IACP set up its field service division in 1960 to conduct modernization surveys of police forces. That year three cities asked to have their departments surveyed. In 1961 the figure rose to five. In 1962 it was fifteen; in 1963, thirteen; and in 1964, twenty-one.

The survey teams give their principal attention to the "Big Five"—recruiting, selection, training, operations, management. While police salary scales and low community prestige continue to pose major obstacles in the way of recruiting, experience has shown that these limitations can be at least partially overcome. Following a survey the Rochester, New York, Police Department launched an intensive recruitment program. The cooperation of leading civic groups was sought and was eagerly given. A program involving news media, displays, literature, and personal contact by policemen and police leaders was instituted for the first time in the city's history. Along with the big recruiting effort, selection and screening standards were sharply raised, and this fact was made known in the recruiting campaign. The effort is paying off; Rochester is getting more and better applicants for its force. So is Chicago, as we have seen; and so is Los Angeles.

The Los Angeles department has requirements for selection and recruiting that are among the nation's highest. "We administer a series of tests to the applicant," says Chief Parker. "One is a written examination to determine mental level and capacity. We also give a physical examination. Then there is an oral examination in which qualified people in the community take part and they make a judgment as to whether this applicant appeals to them as a man who would be a good police officer. The final examination is the psychiatric test given by a leading psychiatrist and his staff from one of our great universities. That test alone eliminates about 10 percent of the individuals who qualify in all other respects. So we start out at least with persons who are apparently well balanced emotionally.

"Then we have an intensive twelve-week training period, during which we create stresses to further test the recruit. There is a weekly evaluation of the recruit by all of his instructors, and eventually the recruits evaluate each other. There is a probationary period of one year from the time the recruit enters the academy so that if at any point he conducts himself improperly, his service can be terminated without a hearing. I think we have every opportunity one could reasonably expect to eliminate the unfit from the police service."

A development which will not only help to solve the training problem, but will also probably do more than anything else to raise prestige, standards, and salaries in the law-enforcement field, is the sudden upsurge of police education in colleges and universities. Northwestern University and the University of California were pioneers in the field; both had programs leading to bachelor of science degrees in criminology and police administration before the Second World War. After the war, other major colleges and universities began to show interest, and since 1960 the movement toward college-level work in police subjects and criminology has gained rapid momentum. Many or most of the students in these programs are working policemen; a smaller but growing number are intelligent young men who are interested in law enforcement as a career.

Typical of the new programs is that of Indiana University, the swift growth of which is described in chapter seven. A similar program was launched in Northeastern University in Boston in 1961. The Northeastern program illustrates the extent to which the college programs are based on the actual training needs of today's police forces. The creator of the program, and its current director, is Robert Sheehan, who has a bachelor's and a master's degree in sociology from Tufts University. While working on his degrees he came in frequent contact with police problems, and his interest in the subject grew.

After discussing with Northeastern the idea of starting a Department of Law Enforcement and Security, and securing its approval, he sent out questionnaires to chiefs of police throughout New England. In these questionnaires he asked which areas of law enforcement might be most usefully covered in such a program, and sought their help and participation in setting up the department. The chiefs were enthusiastic. The areas in which their forces could use intensive training, they said, included interrogation, juvenile problems, crime prevention, and burglary investigation. Courses in each of these subjects were made part of the new department's curriculum, along with courses in detection of forgery, traffic law enforcement, criminal investigation, investigative report writing, and police relations with the public and the community.

The program was begun with courses leading to a bachelor of science or an associate of science (two-year) degree with the major in law enforcement and security. The response has been overwhelming. During the first two years, 800 persons, most of them working policemen from all over New England, have enrolled.

For most of the students the problems involved in taking the courses are very great. In many police departments the chiefs cannot spare more than one or two of their men at a time. In addition, few departments can afford the $44 price tag of a 2-credit, 16-week course. Many of the officers must therefore pay their own way; they can manage it only with great difficulty and personal sacrifice. As the program is becoming better known, civic groups and philanthropists are stepping in to help. In Woburn, Massachusetts, two graduates of the Northeastern courses solved a break-in at the local Sears, Roebuck store in two days. The store manager, learning of the Northeastern program, established two scholarships to enable members of the Woburn force to take the program.

In New Orleans, a group of twenty-one businessmen formed a nonprofit organization called Police Foundation, Inc. The purpose of the foundation is to make every man in the New Orleans police force a college graduate. At present only 12 of the 1,050 men on the force have degrees. Working with the department and with Loyola University, the foundation financed an academic program that was launched by Loyola in the fall of 1963. Eighty-three policemen and six police cadets were the first enrollees in the four-year curriculum. They do not pay for anything, not even their books. The policemen-students attend classes three evenings a week, completing twelve hours a semester, three semesters a year for four years. Meanwhile, both student officers and cadets continue to serve a forty-hour week with the force. Loyola has set up a new criminology department as a major division of the university to handle the program.

In St. Louis a crime research center has been started to study the major problems facing the St. Louis Police Department and departments throughout the United States. The center is under the sponsorship of the Governmental Research Institute and the Social Science Institute of Washington University in St. Louis, and is cosponsored by the St. Louis Police Department. This marks the first time that a crime research center has, in effect, been organized around a police department. Victor B. Brannon, director of the Governmental Research Institute, is chairman of the crime research center's executive committee. Members of the executive committee include Dr. David J. Pittman, associate professor of sociology and psychiatry at Washington University. The first major project to be undertaken by the center will be an intensive study to find out why so few qualified young men seek police work as a career, and what steps can be taken to meet this problem.

New York City plans to launch a four-year police college in 1965, a tuition-free institution that will become the eleventh college in the City University of New York. The curriculum, says that city's Board of Higher Education, will go well beyond professional and technical subjects. It will have a "strong underpinning of liberal arts subjects, stressing the social sciences—history, economics, sociology, anthropology and public administration." All rookies will take a four-month course at the Police Academy, and then will be able to go on for either a two-year curriculum or a four-year curriculum at the Police College, the latter leading to a bachelor of science degree in police studies.

A two-year program in the field has been offered for several years by the City University's Baruch School of Business and Public Administration, with a curriculum including departmental organization, criminalistics, traffic control, juvenile delinquency, and principles of investigation. These courses will be adopted by the Police College as an entity and fitted into the college's broader program. In 1964 about 1,300 New York City policemen were enrolled in the Baruch School's program, and 2,000 or more are expected to enroll in the college. Deputy Chief Inspector George P. McManus, commanding officer of the Police Academy, points out that there are advantages to having a separate college for police. Among other things, it can run on a day-and-night schedule with identical courses being pursued at an identical pace, so that a policeman can shift smoothly from the day to the night classes in mid-semester if his duty hours are changed. Completion of courses and achieving of degrees will be important considerations in the future assignment and promotion of New York City police.

Major philanthropic foundations which, along with the academic community, long ignored law enforcement as a field of activity, are beginning to sponsor programs to improve American police forces. The Ford Foundation made five awards in 1964 to help strengthen the standards of police administration "through selective nationally significant training and research programs." The grants were to the International Association of Chiefs of Police, $400,000; the Southwestern Police Institute, $500,000; Northwestern University Law School, $300,000; University of Wisconsin Law School, $260,000; and the Institute of Judicial Administration of New York University School of Law, $266,000. These grants marked the first major activity in the field of police work by the nation's largest foundation.

Such developments hold promise. But there remain many formidable obstacles to the elimination of police corruption. One of them is the nation's gambling laws. Gambling is our present-day Prohibition, and one of our greatest law-making dilemmas. A large percentage of America's population does not regard it as immoral. In one state, Nevada, it is perfectly legal. In the others, most forms of gambling are not legal. In these other forty-nine states it is the largest single source of revenue for the nation's crime syndicates, and is probably the largest single corrupter of the police.

Public contempt for the law is bred by the outlawing of things that people do not believe to be wrong. It is further aggravated by inconsistencies in the law that deprive it of such moral basis as it might have had. "Who says it's all right to gamble on bingo in church but wrong to bet on a number at home?" exclaimed one New York housewife when the city's 1964 police-gambling scandal broke. In 1957 the people of New York State had voted in a referendum, by a nearly two-to-one margin, to amend the anti-gambling article in the state constitution to permit bingo games under church and charity auspices. In New York City people voted nearly three-to-one for legalization of off-track betting on a 1963 referendum (this referendum was advisory only; off-track betting is still illegal in the city). The inconsistency between legal bingo and the illegal numbers game has made the gambling laws a subject of widespread ridicule in New York. *The New York Times* editorialized: ". . . while graft in the Police Department must be rigorously cleaned out—and District Attorney Hogan and Commissioner Murphy can be depended on to follow through—the real corrupter is not gambling per se but the gambling laws themselves."

Legalizing gambling in the United States and subjecting it to proper control is a proposal that is often made. Proponents state that it would cut organized crime off from a major source of income; raise U.S. tax revenues by bringing the billion-dollar gambling industry within the legitimate, taxable stream of commerce; remove from the books a set of laws that brings the law itself into ridicule and contempt; and cut off a major source of police corruption.

Interestingly enough, several distinguished criminologists are on record in opposition to legalized gambling, including Superintendent Wilson of Chicago and Virgil W. Peterson, operating director of the Chicago Crime Commission. "Gambling," said Peterson, in a letter written to *The New York Times* on July 10, 1964, "is a corrupting influence and this is true whether it is legal or illegal.

Legalization of gambling greatly increases the volume of gambling and thus spreads the economic and social evils that always attend widespread gambling." On the subject of the relationship of gambling to police corruption, he stated, "Police corruption is certainly not confined to the enforcement of gambling laws. Some of America's biggest police scandals in recent years—i.e., Chicago, Denver—stemmed from burglary law enforcement. Enforcement of liquor and traffic laws has been notoriously corrupt in many places."

Americans, he added, should not glibly assume from the fact that the British have recently legalized gambling that the British experience is proving such legalization to be wise. On April 30, 1964, Arthur L. Goodhart, professor of jurisprudence and Fellow of University College, Oxford, who is also chairman of the International Law Association and a member of the Royal Commission to the Police, discussed the British situation in an address in Chicago. He mentioned the success that England had achieved in combating commercialized prostitution. "But," he added, "the law has proved to be far less successful in its control of gambling. . . . Those who were influenced by this perfervid egalitarianism did not stop to think that it might be more serious for a poor man, and especially for his family, to lose money on bets than it was for a wealthy one. Unfortunately, Parliament . . . in 1960 . . . enacted the Betting and Gambling Act, which has made legal almost all forms of gambling. The wave of gambling that has spread over the whole country has proved to be far greater than anyone expected. The moral and economic consequences of this freedom to gamble are only beginning to show. . . ."

With these arguments and citations, Mr. Peterson has presented the full case against legalized gambling as it is usually set forth. One cannot help but applaud the thought with which he ends his *Times* letter: "Easy solutions to difficult social problems are usually deceptive." In the face of this heavy weight of authority and the important considerations set forth by Mr. Peterson, it is nevertheless hard to escape the conclusion that the legalization of gambling must be considered in the United States.

The arguments that gambling is a "corrupting influence . . . whether it is legal or illegal," that legalization will greatly increase the scope of the activity, and that the poor and their families will be harmed, are the same arguments that were used to fight the repeal of Prohibition. The country, however, ultimately came to the conclusion that the first of these three points was overdone, that the second was not all that terrible, and the third, while inescapably true, was a problem of less magnitude than was supposed by the "drys." Opposed to such weight as the combined merit of these three points could muster was the all-but-universal contempt for the law, the financial bonanza for organized crime, and widespread corruption of the police that stemmed from Prohibition. Few people today would contend that the repeal of Prohibition was ill-advised. It is not easy to see why the scales of public wisdom should tip differently when the same tests are applied to gambling.

On the question of police corruption, Mr. Peterson may be touching on this issue too lightly by pointing out that not all police scandals stem from gambling. The fact is that many, probably most, police scandals do. As much as half the existing police graft and payoffs in the United States would probably cease on the day that gambling was legalized and put under proper supervision. Under the circumstances, the British experience with legalized gambling should be fully and carefully studied in this country, and a dialogue should begin on the question of repealing this present-day form of Prohibition.

This leaves one other major issue—the attitude of the American community toward the police, and its impact on corruption. In the Preface I stated that this is not a book about bad police in a virtuous society, and I believe that the chapters of the book have given documentation for that point of view. I stated that I consider blanket condemnations of police to tell a lot more about the condemners than they do about the police, and I hope I have proved that too.

Actually, Americans are a race of great and remarkably honest self-criticizers. The issue of public responsibility for police shortcomings has been getting a lot of discussion since the new wave of police scandals broke. People listened soberly to the salty grousing of Chief Parker of Los Angeles on the reasons for the difficulty in obtaining good policemen: "I think it is because of the general treatment accorded the police service by the American public. On the one hand, the public has made it extremely difficult for the police officers to work in a favorable atmosphere; on the other hand, the public has expected phenomenal results from a police force working against odds."

When the Denver scandal broke, the Washington, D.C., *Post* took up the cudgels for the police, and planted some well-placed welts on the public pate:

The police scandal in Denver raises some grim questions for the rest of the country. Are law enforcement agencies in other cities shot through with comparable corruption? Are metropolitan police departments anywhere in the United States dealt with fairly enough, generously enough, and wisely enough to avoid such corruption?

Policemen are expected to be knights errant, fearless in the face of danger, incorruptible in the midst of corruption, cool and knowledgeable in the determination of constitutional questions over which learned judges may reflect and wrangle and divide. They are supposed to be tough on criminals but tender regarding the rights of individuals, minority groups, and the innocent generally. They are asked to be incessantly courteous, kind and cheerful—and to be ready to lay down their lives at any moment if need be in the defense of law and order.

To attract such paragons, most American communities offer only miserably low pay scales, long working hours and something close to a sneer from the public. Often, policemen have been obliged, as in New York for example, to take a variety of outside jobs, most of them rather menial, in order to support their families in minimum decency. The practice is called "moonlighting" and it is all too likely to lead to lawlessness, or at the very least to petty graft.

If the police in special situations such as Denver and Chicago have on occasion mistreated the American public, the American public has, by and large, grievously mistreated the police. Cities are likely to get just about the level of law enforcement they want and are willing to pay for. They need drastically to raise their sights if they want to raise the caliber, integrity, morale, and efficiency of their police forces.

The public took another couple of welts from a veteran clobberer that it adores, Margaret Mead. Anthropologist Mead wrote a letter to *The New York Times* on June 18, 1964, following a wave of crimes and violence in the city. "As long as we continue to see the police as the natural enemies of law-abiding citizens and law breakers alike, we shall continue to struggle helplessly with the multiple effects of low trust, diffuse hostility, and defeatist attitudes," she said. "A responsible police force—the enemies of crime and danger and the protectors of all people—depends on trust and is an essential safeguard in a complex society."

The people—who, after the professionals and the reformers and the universities and the decent cops have done all they can, hold the final key to "a responsible police force"—bowed their heads and listened. But it remains to be seen how much of the lesson America has really accepted and understood.

Index